Essays and Studies 1988

The English Association

The object of the English Association is to promote understanding and appreciation of the English language and its literature.

The Association is an international organization with branches at home and overseas. Its activities include sponsoring a number of publications and organizing conferences, seminars, and group discussions, including annual sixth-form conferences and the London Graduate Student Seminar.

Publications

The Year's Work in English Studies. An annual bibliographical survey of scholarly books and articles on English, American, and Commonwealth Literature and Language. Published by John Murray (USA: Humanities Press).

Essays and Studies. An annual anthology of essays usually on a wide range of subjects from the medieval to the modern. A collector is nominated every year by the Association. Published by John Murray (USA: Humanities Press).

English. The journal of the Association, *English* is published three times a year by the Oxford University Press.

News-Letter. A *News-Letter* is issued three times a year giving information about forthcoming publications, conferences, and other activities.

Occasional Publications. The Association has published or sponsored many occasional works including *A Guide to Degree Courses in English* (sixth edition 1982), *English Grammar For Today*, *English Short Stories of Today*, *Poems of Today*, and many pamphlets.

Membership

For details write to The Secretary, The English Association, 1 Priory Gardens, London W4 1TT.

Essays and Studies 1988

MATTHEW ARNOLD 1988: A CENTENNIAL REVIEW

Edited by
Miriam Allott

for the English Association

JOHN MURRAY, LONDON
HUMANITIES PRESS,
ATLANTIC HIGHLANDS, NJ

ESSAYS AND STUDIES 1988
IS VOLUME FORTY-ONE IN THE NEW SERIES
OF ESSAYS AND STUDIES COLLECTED ON BEHALF OF
THE ENGLISH ASSOCIATION

© The English Association 1988
First published 1988
by John Murray (Publishers) Ltd
50 Albemarle Street, London W1X 4BD

Typeset by Colset Private Limited, Singapore
Printed and bound in Great Britain by
Mackays of Chatham PLC, Chatham, Kent

British Library Cataloguing in Publication Data

Essays and studies: Matthew Arnold, a centennial
 review.——Vol. 41 (1988)
  1. English literature – Critical studies
  – Serials
  I. English Association
  820.9

ISBN 0-7195-4562-5
ISBN 0-7195-4563-3 Pb

First published 1988 in the United States of America by
HUMANITIES PRESS INTERNATIONAL, INC.,
Atlantic Highlands, NJ 07716

The Library of Congress has cataloged this serial
publication as follows:

Essays and studies (London, England: 1950)
Essays and studies: being volume 41 of the new series of essays
and studies collected for the English Association. — 1950-
— London: J. Murray, [1950-

v.: ill.; 22 cm.

Annual.
Title varies slightly.
Vols. for 1950–1981 called also new ser., v. 3-v. 34.
Continues: English studies (London, England)

1. English literature—History and criticism. 2. English philology—Collections.
 I. English Association. II. Title. III. Title: Essays & studies.
        PR13.E4   820.4   36-8431
        AACR 2 MARC-S

Library of Congress   [8509r85]rev5

ISBN 0-391-03587-8

Contents

Abbreviations

Biographical Note

Matthew Arnold: Born Laleham-on-Thames, 24 December 1822; died Liverpool, 15 April 1888, of heart failure, while awaiting the arrival of his married daughter from America. Son of the Reverend Thomas Arnold (headmaster of Rugby School from 1828 until his death in 1842) and Mary Arnold (née Penrose). Winchester School, 1836–7; Rugby School, 1837–40; Balliol College, Oxford, 1841–4. Temporary assistant master at Rugby; elected Fellow of Oriel College, Oxford, 1845. Private secretary to the Marquis of Lansdowne, Lord President of the Council, 1847–50. Appointed Inspector of Schools, 15 April 1851; Senior Inspector of Schools, 1870; Chief Inspector of Schools, 1884; retired 30 April 1886. Married Frances Lucy, daughter of Sir William Wightman, Justice of the Queen's Bench, June 1851. Elected Professor of Poetry at Oxford, 5 May 1853. Foreign Assistant Commissioner to the Newcastle Commission on Elementary Education, 1859, travelling in France, Holland, and Switzerland; Foreign Assistant Commissioner to the Taunton (*Schools Enquiry*) Commission, April–November 1865, travelling in France, Italy, Germany, and Switzerland. Risked official hostility by publishing in *Fraser's Magazine* 'The Twice-Revised Code', an attack on Robert Lowe's new method of distributing government grants for education ('Payment by Results'), March 1862. Honorary DCL at Oxford, 1870. Declined re-nomination for the Professorship of Poetry at Oxford, and for the Lord Rectorship at St Andrews University, February and November 1877. Accepted Civil List pension of £250 a year 'in public recognition of service to the poetry and literature of England', August 1883. First visit to America, on a six-month lecture-tour, October 1883–March 1884 (*Discourses in America* published June 1885). Again declined re-nomination for the Professorship of Poetry at Oxford, though touched by memorials from heads of colleges, tutors, and four hundred undergraduates. Visited Germany for the Royal Commission on Education, June, November, and December 1885. Again visited France, Switzerland, and Germany for the Royal Commission on Education. Second visit to America, February–March, May–August 1886. Prose works reprinted in chronological order in R. H. Super's *The Complete Prose Works of Matthew Arnold*, eleven volumes (Ann Arbor: University of Michigan Press, 1960–77). Poetical works reprinted in chronological order in *The Poems of Matthew Arnold*, Longman's Annotated Poets, edited by Kenneth Allott (1965), second edition by Miriam Allott (1979). New chronological edition with full textual and critical commentary, *Matthew Arnold: Complete Poetical Works*, edited by Miriam Allott and Nicholas Shrimpton, forthcoming from Oxford University Press. Professor Cecil Y. Lang's complete edition of Arnold's letters due to appear in the early 1990s.

Introduction

MIRIAM ALLOTT

'The inseparable propriety of time,' declared Francis Bacon, 'is ever more and more to disclose truth.' The notion is appealing for anyone introducing a collection of essays written to commemorate an author one hundred years after his death. It was a favourite idea with Matthew Arnold, too. He uses the original Greek saying (traditionally attributed to the philosopher Thales) as his motto for *Empedocles on Etna, and Other Poems* (1852), and many years later, in *Literature and Dogma* (1873), he is found using it again, this time in his own translation, 'Time is the wisest of all things for he is the unfailing discoverer.'[1] His trust in the idea underlies the famous pronouncement about the status of his own work, made when he was virtually at the end of his career as a poet and already launched on his career as a writer of prose: 'It is very animating to think one at last has the chance of *getting at* the English public,' he had said in 1863, 'Such a public it is, and such a work as one wants to do with it!'[2] Six years later, in June of 1869, when the two-volume collection of his poems was about to appear, he set out the celebrated little survey of himself in his letter to his mother, that much-loved and confided-in figure who had been Dr. Arnold's widow then for twenty-seven years:

> My poems represent, on the whole, the main movement of mind of the last quarter of a century, and thus they will probably have their day as people become conscious to themselves of what that movement of mind is, and interested in the literary productions which reflect it. It may be fairly urged that I have less poetical sentiment than Tennyson, and less intellectual vigour and abundance than Browning; yet, because I have perhaps more of a fusion of the two than either of them, and have more regularly applied that fusion to the main line of modern development, I am likely enough to have my turn as they have had theirs.[3]

One of the essays in this collection—Nicholas Shrimpton's 'Arnold and the Movement of Mind: The Four States of "In Utrumque Paratus" '—takes the first part of this passage as its text, arguing from Arnold's changes in a particular poem over the years that such alterations may indeed serve as a practical illustration of the way in which his poetry can reflect a particular movement of mind at work in his age. Time, then, has in this case disclosed at least a fresh perspective on Arnold in *his* time, highlighting, as the essay suggests, certain ineluctable links between text and context.

As it turns out, all the essays in this volume engage themselves, directly or indirectly, with this matter. It was not intended to hold contributions either to a programme of topics covering 'aspects of Arnold' in a suitably comprehensive, celebratory manner, or to try for a series of conscious 'revaluations'. The essays here are exclusively the expression of their authors' particular Arnoldian interests and concerns. For the collector, what was striking, as the essays came in, was the diversity of theme and approach combined with the steady eye in each case on the centrality of Arnold's concerns for his own time, and by extension for ours. Judging by the emphasis on such continuities in these essays of the late 1980s, time also seems busy confirming a prophetic truth in Arnold's 1869 pronouncement about himself.

It is the case that his reputation did not capsize as dramatically as those of some of his fellow Great Victorians in the post-Strachey period; it did not do so because, for reasons he recognized and understood, he was never so widely popular. But his 'turn' has to do with something more than his not falling into the Edwardian trough with Tennyson and Browning and George Eliot. Such major Victorians were in any case to be recalled to immensely vigorous life, especially from the 1940s onwards, as any English exam syllabus will readily testify. But Arnold did not then remain 'ahead' with them ('The rumour is that you are ahead', he was told while awaiting the results of the election for the Professorship of Poetry at Oxford in May 1857). If he was represented at all in the 'canon', this would be with one or two pieces, among them perhaps 'Dover Beach' or 'The Scholar-Gipsy' or 'Thyrsis' or 'Sohrab and Rustum'. *Empedocles on Etna*, his major long poem—perhaps the age's major long poem—is even yet omitted, astonishingly, from the newest edition of the *Oxford Book of Victorian Verse*. It seems fair to say, too, that he still remains virtually unknown to the general reader as a prose writer, apart, that is, from the seminal essay on Wordsworth (which was responsible for establishing our habit of distinguishing the qualities of Wordsworth's earlier from those of his later work), and the little occasional piece, 'The Study of Poetry', also written in the 1880s and thus towards the end of his life, which was designed as an introduction for T. H. Ward's popular

anthology, *The English Poets*.[4] This is the essay on which so much
critical weight has so extraordinarily been laid, extraordinarily, that
is, when one considers its relation to the vast quantity of important
writing reprinted in Robert Super's masterly edition of Arnold's *Complete Prose Works*, with which many of us have really not much more
than a nodding acquaintance, and with only part of which—given the
amount there is—even the most devoted scholar is likely to be closely
familiar. In the present collection, Brian Nellist's 'Disconcerting the
Reader: *Friendship's Garland* and the True Voices of "Mr. Arnold",'
goes a long way, an admirable distance indeed, considering the economy of space, towards redressing an imbalance. It reaches out from
and returns to its starting-point in *Friendship's Garland*, probably the
most sustained instance of what Arnold called his 'vivacities'—
ruefully, since it was clear that his 'English public' did not as a rule like
the play of irony, finding it incompatible with being 'wholly serious',
the phrase slyly attributed in Max Beerbohm's famous cartoon to
Arnold's small, prim niece, who grew up into the prestigious Mrs.
Humphry Ward, author of *Robert Elsmere*. 'Why oh why, Uncle Matt,'
he has her ask the elongated figure leaning against the mantelpiece,
'will you never be wholly serious?'.

The essay on *Friendship's Garland*, in common with John Farrell's
'"What You Feel, I Share": Breaking the Dialogue of the Mind with
Itself' (the quotation is from one of Arnold's five 1848 debating sonnets addressed to his friend Arthur Hugh Clough), recognizes as
fundamental in Arnold's creative procedures the interplay of different
voices. What we begin to see in these essays, as elsewhere in this
volume, is that Arnold's 'turn' depends on a growing recognition of
the continuity of many of his principal preoccupations and procedures
with our own. T. S. Eliot, we remember, originally chose 'He do the
Police in Different Voices' as the title for *The Waste Land*; and the
image captured in his final title applies not only to his own portrayal of
a state of being to which the modern sensibility finds itself particularly
vulnerable, but also to Arnold's picture of the present-day world 'with
its sick hurry, its divided aims' from which he bids his scholar-gipsy
fly, '. . . fly our paths, our feverish contact fly!' Arnold's use of
'different voices' in his poetry derives from that sustained exploratory
dialogue of the mind with itself which in his 1853 Preface he specifically associates with the modern spirit (though, as Farrell points out,
the dialogue is with other minds as well)[5]; in his prose it is the mode
adopted by a flexible critical spirit engaged, as Nellist says, to demonstrate 'through the variations and shifts of voice . . . that even more

important than the several issues discussed is a temper of mind with
which they should be all addressed' (p. 31).

   This insight is an urgently needed corrective. It is a sad fact that to
the extent—and it is considerable—that Arnold has become a subject
of academic study, he can be served as ill by his friends as by his
enemies, especially, perhaps, on this side of the Atlantic. One of the
means by which Arnold began to get a 'turn' of sorts was through
the immense modern proliferation of scholarly and critical work on
nineteenth-century writers. In the many published records of such
work, the number of pages devoted to overviews of recent Arnold
studies in, for example, the PMLA *Guides to Research* and the regular
surveys produced by major American specialist periodicals such as
Victorian Poetry and *The Arnoldian: A Review of Mid-Victorian Culture*,
constitute overwhelming evidence of the vast amount of research
devoted to his work in prose and verse, an amount certainly equal to, if
not sometimes exceeding, the amount devoted to the two poets with
whom he compared himself in 1869. The sources referred to, it will be
noted, are American. So is the vast majority of the work done, and
quantity here is not inconsistent with quality. It does seem true to say
that in this American work there is less of the kind of intellectual unease
which Arnold seems to generate in this country. He would probably
see a continuation of the parochialism he took arms against in the
cautious, latter-day defensiveness sometimes found in English inter-
pretations of his critical stance in relation to education, literature,
religion, and politics. The tone in some instances seems to hint at a
good deal of nervous glancing over the shoulder to ward off ideological
hosts of Midian, prowling around ready to pounce. If they do pounce,
the target as often as not is a rather pounceable-upon figure, the
product of a misguided, if well-intentioned, quasi-Leavisian liberal
and 'safe' reading of a writer who, whatever he was, and whatever his
limitations, was certainly not that.

   But time, all the same, seems to be doing its 'proprietal' best to
disclose less tangential truths about this writer. It is in keeping with the
movements of mind and sensibility explored in the three essays I have
referred to that the remaining four essays in this collection should
further illustrate the diversity of Arnold's range, whether as a writer or
in his professional life as an Inspector of Schools; and that in doing so
they should reveal at how many points he touches his own time and
ours. All ages are of course ages of transition, but Philip Davis's
'Arnold's Gift: The Poet in an Unpoetic Age' distinguishes the special

plight of a creative intelligence finding itself, in the celebrated lines from 'Stanzas from the Grande Chartreuse',

> Wandering between two worlds, one dead,
> The other powerless to be born . . . (ll. 85–6)

—the dead world being the world of orthodox beliefs and certainties, the one not yet born being the world of scientific truths and demythologized religion. In this reading, the poet's position 'between two worlds', with his attendant need somehow to master, as Davis says, 'personal helplessness' (pp. 68–9) and find a voice adequate to his own and the age's need, looks back to Wordsworth and forward through Hardy to ourselves. The essay's concern with the connection between the writer's predicament then and now is suggested in its title, which echoes another title, *Humboldt's Gift*, chosen by the modern American author, Saul Bellow, for his novel about a writer struggling against personal discouragement and the corrosive sense of belonging to an age out of joint and unfavourable to a talent seemingly ill-fitted to help to set it right.

Arnold, as we know, did not sink under all this, being as a man, if not as a poet, really quite extraordinarily tough and resilient. Not so extraordinarily, perhaps, for he remained in many ways his father's son, a 'sound' Victorian, determined, like the harassed cleric in M. R. James's famous story, to remain 'firm' in the face of all the darknesses crouching at the door. He was buoyed up through trials and tribulations, as well as through the ordinary fatigues and pressures of a hard-working professional career, partly by fortifying himself with the writers who 'propped his mind in these bad days',[6] and partly by keeping himself open to the still powerful presence in his life of Thomas Arnold, that strong, eupeptic marshaller of the talents and duties of his large and affectionate family who was also to become, in the years up to his early death in 1842, the abiding lodestar for several generations of Rugby schoolboys. But if Arnold did not succumb, turning zestfully in the 1860s to the business of pulling out 'a few more stops in that powerful but at present somewhat narrow-toned organ, the modern Englishman'[7], he nevertheless chose as the central figure for his major long poem, composed at the beginning of the 1850s, the Greek philosopher Empedocles, born in the time out of joint after the great age of fifth-century Greece, who, conscious of loss of buoyancy and troubled by some 'root of suffering in himself,/Some secret and unfollowed vein of woe'[8], casts himself—though even so expressing a sense of exultation at rejoining the natural elements from which he came—into Etna's volcanic crater. In 'Empedocles and Byron Once More', Bernard Beatty seizes upon the fortuitous coincidence of the centenary of Arnold's death with the bicentenary of Byron's birth to explore the ambiguities of Arnold's lifelong feeling for Byron, linking the 'Titanism' which Arnold ascribes to him with an envied Promethean figure sensed to be lurking, so to speak, in the sub-text of Arnold's poetic drama—a drama which, it is known, owes at least some elements of its formal structure to Byron's *Manfred*.

This discussion complements Farrell's in ' "What You Feel, I Share" . . .' which underlines Arnold's urgent initiation of his dialogue with Senancour in the interests of exorcising Byron's troubling presence. Each essay makes its own contribution to the prolonged debate about Arnold's dissent from, yet indissociable relationship with, the mood and temper of romanticism in general and the romantic poets in particular. The *locus classicus* in his own debate with himself about the poet's duty to follow classic principles is the Preface of 1853, which tries to explain why he dropped *Empedocles on Etna* from this second edition of his 1852 collection; it was replaced by what he felt to be the more 'animating' and ennobling 'Sohrab and Rustum'. The Preface, if it were remarkable for nothing else, would be remembered for the special distinction of having satisfied nobody from the day it first appeared. But the point is that Empedocles gives dramatic expression to one of the most sombre of 'Mr Arnold's' various voices (too 'morbid' said the Preface, hence the dismissal),[9] just as Empedocles's counterpart, Callicles, gives expression to the equally characteristic and complex lyrical-elegiac voice we are perhaps most familiar with from the famous poems 'Dover Beach', 'The Scholar-Gipsy' and 'Thyrsis'.

Ruth apRoberts in 'Matthew Arnold and George Sand' reminds us of yet another voice—or, more accurately, two more voices. The first is that of the youthfully romantic enthusiast of the 1840s, who in those 'days of Lélia', still warmly remembered in his commemorative essay written after George Sand's death in 1876,[10] fell heavily for all things French, followed Rachel's stage performances with the passion of a fan for a favourite pop star, and became deeply entangled emotionally with a girl we know from his 'Switzerland' poems as 'Marguerite'. 'Matt is full of Parisianism,' wrote Clough in a much-quoted letter just after Arnold had returned to Oxford from his visit to France in the winter of 1846 to 1847, theatres in general, and Rachel in special: he enters a room with a chanson of Beranger's on his lips—for the sake of French words almost conscious of tune: his carriage shows him in fancy parading the rue de Rivoli;—and his hair is guiltless of English scissors: he breakfasts at twelve, and never dines in Hall, and in the week or 8 days rather (for 2 Sundays must be included) he has been to Chapel *once*. . .[11]

The essay traces the ardent response to George Sand of this 'Milton jeune et voygeant', as George Sand herself saw him when he made his pilgrimage to her home at Nohant (p. 97). She remained a vivid memory for him through the years. 'George Sand,' says Lionel Trilling in what is still one of the most intelligent books about Arnold, 'had begun her life in revolt—against stupidity, against prudence, convention, aridity. Revolt passed away but not the sentiment that had always animated her: "the sentiment of the ideal life, which is none other than man's normal life as we shall one day know it" [the passage quoted is from Arnold's own late commemorative essay]. If, with this sentiment, George Sand had fired his youth, with it she also fortified his age.'[12] What the present essay does is to invite us to listen to yet another voice, in this case the voice of a particular kind of religious longing which may have made the Arnold of the 1840s especially interested in George Sand's *Spiridion*. Though we are not certain he read it then, this longing certainly sent him back to it in 1882, six years before his death, when he copied out so many extracts from the novel, and also from the 'eternal gospel' set forth by Joachim of Flora, which in George Sand's novel is discovered by Spiridion and becomes the centre of his spiritual biography (pp. 104–6). This is the gospel which preaches 'a new revelation, a new religion, a new society, a new humanity', and while preserving Christianity, 'will do away with the forms. . . .' This 'éternel évangile' was admired, along with the revolutionary *Spiridion*, by Renan, whose writings were themselves much admired by Arnold; his notebooks contain many extracts from them as well. The Arnold whose voice is remembered in the essay on George Sand is the author of *God and the Bible* and (Arnold's one best-seller) *Literature and Dogma*, the religious writings to which he devoted himself in the 1870s and in which, while Christianity is firmly 'preserved', what are emphatically repudiated are, on the one hand, the conception of a personal god and, on the other, the possibility of miracle.[13]

When he compared himself with Tennyson and Browning in 1869,

Arnold could have added that he was separated from them not only by the wider range of subject matter, which, as a lecturer and essayist, he was able to explore throughout his life, but also by the necessity to earn his own living. Tennyson's financial difficulties were eased by the award of a Civil List pension; Browning and his wife, with the help of a legacy, were able to live abroad in Florence. Arnold, strapped for money from the beginning, was obliged to find work before he was in a position to marry the girl he began to pay court to in 1850. After coming down from Oxford, from 1847 to 1851 he acted as private secretary to the Marquis of Lansdowne, and in this period, some time between 1847 and 1849, he underwent his 'éducation sentimentale', if that is how we may describe the experiences recorded in the 'Marguerite' poems. These he gathered in the series he called 'Switzer-land', where the central themes are those of loss and separation.[14] 'Faded Leaves', his second series of love poems, was inspired by Frances Lucy Wightman, whom he won permission to marry—from her father, Justice Wightman—only when he had secured with the help of Lord Lansdowne the work he would be held to all his life. In April 1851 he was appointed Inspector of Schools; on June 10 he married; from September to October he took a delayed honeymoon on the Continent, travelling in France, Italy, and Switzerland, and visit-ing the Grande Chartreuse, which inspired one of his most important earlier poems.

In October Arnold finally started work as a school inspector, and so he remained from that time until his retirement in 1886. Two years before he retired in 1884, he rose to the position of Chief Inspector of Schools; two years after he retired, on 15 April 1888, he died of a heart attack while awaiting at Liverpool the arrival of his daughter and her husband from America. 'What did Arnold do for thirty-five years in that grinding job in Her Majesty's Government?' asks Vincent Tollers in his essay, 'A Working Isaiah: Arnold in the Council Office', and what he offers in reply supports his central contention. 'Under Queen Victoria,' he says, 'education became one of England's primary enterprises, and Arnold was at its geographical and political centre (p. 114).' Even the brief biographical note presented elsewhere in this volume (p. vii) suggests that Arnold's work in education would be enough by itself for any full-time career. This essay on his educational life underlines not only the amount of work he had to do as part of his everyday routine, but also the strong practical and political influence he tried to bring to bear on problems to which—in the present time of considerable crisis in all levels of our educational system—we are still trying to bring some kind of resolution. Tollers is properly concerned, too, with Arnold's energetic involvement in these problems. We sometimes remember only the sense of constriction and frustration he expresses in some of his poems and letters, perhaps especially in the 1860s, when he was so often fatigued with his regular journeys of inspection to schools round the country, his one-night stops in dreary hotels, and his separation from Frances Lucy and their growing family of children—which was especially difficult, for he was as deeply bound by domestic affections and family ties as his father had been. 'I sometimes cry for air, like my own Empedocles,' he said once, and images of imprisonment and constriction multiply in his 1860s sonnets, where we sense him fighting with all his resources to be 'firm' (one of these, 'The Better Part', was in fact originally entitled 'Anti-Desperation')[15]. These resources included a new familiarity with the writings of Marcus Aurelius, a figure whose own plangent facing-up to moral trouble and the heaviness of office added to Arnold's feeling for the Stoic position which he had earlier encountered in his reading of the Greek philosophers.[16] He describes ruefully, in a letter of 1864, his occupation of hearing students give lessons:

> Here is my programme for this afternoon: Avalanches—The Steam Engine—The Thames—India Rubber—Bricks—The Battle of Poitiers—Subtraction—The Reindeer—The Gunpowder Plot—The Jordan. Alluring is it not? Twenty minutes each, and the days of one's life are only threescore years and ten.[17]

'. . . It is pain and grief composing with such interruptions as I have,' he had told Clough some ten years earlier, in 1853.[18] We must remember that while earning his living in this way he was also preparing his Oxford lectures, knocking them into shape for publication, and writing more and more frequently on public issues for magazines and periodicals. And trying to write poetry. The reasons for the brevity of his poetic career—it lasted little more than ten years—have been discussed often elsewhere; they are many and complex, but these circumstances certainly played their part.

But whatever the price paid for this unceasingly heavy load of work, the great consequence, as Tollers's essay helps to show, was that Arnold gained a closer familiarity than almost any of his literary contemporaries with the everyday life of ordinary people around the country, and indeed abroad as well. Moreover, his sense of his times covered a wide spectrum of different classes and kinds of men and women. His periodic visits of inspection to schools were looked forward to by more than one hard-pressed and isolated teacher who liked good talk and congenial company; and on his tours abroad for his various educational commissions he was equally at ease in putting into service the ideas of leading figures of the day: among others in France, for instance, he met Guizot, Villemain, Victor Cousin, and the Duc de Broglie, whose writings he frequently cites in his reports. In 1865, more than a century before British television documentaries on education have tried to draw the same comparisons, he wrote of the importance of European secondary education. He found 'no countries more worth studying, as regards secondary education, than those in which intellectual life has been carried furthest—Germany first, and, in the second degree, France,' and he worked to the end that 'England may run well in this race.' The importance of his book on European education, *Schools and Universities on the Continent* (1868), is stressed by Robert Super: 'It is not likely,' he says in his commentary on this work, 'that anyone who has a curiosity about European education in the nineteenth century—in itself or as a background to modern education—can find a more lucid, intelligent account than this book, nor is there a better statement of the aim of liberal education . . .'[19]

This practical-minded, hard-working, intelligent man has not, I think, as yet been understood quite in the way that seems consonant with his peculiar gifts. Perhaps the most hindering influence has been the enormous diversity of his efforts; he was engaged in so many different ways, personal and public, with times which he felt were out of joint, and which his missionary sense told him he should make the best use of his gifts to try to set right. In possessing and trying to follow this sense, he was—as in so many other ways—absolutely a man of his day. But some contemporary literary figures were perhaps more fortunate than the Arnold who was a poet, in that their creative gifts marvellously matched this compelling principle. George Eliot, with whom Arnold has a great deal in common, is an outstanding example. But his native muse, essentially elegiac, introspective, melancholy, required 'an actual tearing of oneself to pieces', as he told his favourite sister, if one was to get the work anywhere near right.[20] A muse thus at odds with what he took to be the need of the age for something more invigorating than 'pleasing melancholy',[21] and at the same time too exigent for energies depleted by other activities, had either to be placed under different orders or bidden farewell. In the end it was she who abandoned him (muses are by tradition female), but not before she had been pressed into the service of a more public kind of poetry in which the struggle for formal perfection was taken on because it was felt to be less arduous than the struggle to 'get breast to breast with reality' in the more private kind.[22] His subjugated muse helped him before the end to achieve 'Sohrab and Rustum' and 'Balder Dead', with its moving theme from Norse legend, and, in relation to what was being tried for, its fairly honourable defeat.

In prose writing, Arnold's missionary sense found at its service the different, lively, polemical gifts lighted up for us in Brian Nellist's reflections on *Friendship's Garland*. But even here his individual qualities and strengths worked against his winning popular sympathy in his own time and ours, and for much the same reasons. He engaged zestfully, and over a wide front, with public matters, and did so largely in a medium which was equivalent to today's popular journalism. But he did not do so in the full-fronted way that pleases and reassures. He used irony and wit in the interests of encouraging a particular stance in the face of what he felt were dangerous and complicated difficulties and prejudices, and also as a salute to, and a means of awakening, a sense of precisely such complexities. But in ages hot for certainties, the heat increasing with the distance to which certainties recede, this rarely goes down well. Moreover, his zest meant that he wrote a great deal, much of it in response to debating points he had himself stimulated. New readers often arrive, so to speak, in the middle of an argument, where a particular issue, and as often as not a particular kind of simplification, is being engaged with, and perhaps ironically bounced up and down. This in turn means that the important polarities between which Arnold moves as a thinker, and which promote his own 'dialogue of the mind with itself' as well as his engagement with others, may thus escape attention. With any luck, though, even a reader so placed may be made aware of the genuine play of intelligence: '. . . how glad I am to find/On any page the least display of mind' runs the closing passage on this rare commodity in Robert Frost's wry little poem, 'A Considerable Speck'.

Those engaged in commemorating Arnold's work in this centennial year, whether in discussions such as these in the present volume, or in investigative conferences here and abroad,[23] have the hope that time will at least now begin to disclose to more people than before that Arnold's kind of intelligence is worth engaging with, if for no other reason than that it frames questions that still need framing, and goes some way towards indicating that so far as our cultural, spiritual, and political health is concerned, the answers may lie as much in the manner in which such questions are framed, and addressed, as in anything else. Arnold felt something like this, too, but was not at the time sanguine that others would agree: '. . . what the English public cannot understand,' he said, 'is that a man can be a just and fruitful object of contemplation much more by virtue of what spirit he is of than by what system of doctrine he elaborates . . .'[24] Some modern readers, who for this reason find Arnold himself 'a just and fruitful object of contemplation,' add the essential point that 'spirit' is not detached from content ('How the work is written is the major part of what is said,' says Nellist of *Friendship's Garland*). This is the main key to the procedures informing Arnold's 'criticism of life', and ultimately helps to explain how 'criticism' and 'culture', as he uses these terms, come at last to be seen as one and the same.

Notes

[1] *CPW* vi 265.

[2] Letter to his mother, 29 October 1863 (*Letters* i 201).

[3] Letter to his mother, 5 June 1869 (*Letters* ii 9).

[4] T. H. Ward, the husband of Arnold's niece Mary, published his four volumes of *The English Poets* (1880–81), with critical introductions by various writers. Arnold contributed the General Introduction and introductory notes on Gray and Keats (all written during 1880).

[5] Preface to first edition of *Poems* (1853) (*CPW* i 1).

[6] For some of these writers see, e.g., the references to Epictetus, Homer, and Sophocles in Arnold's 1848 sonnet 'To a Friend', beginning (rather clumsily), 'Who prop, thou ask'st, in these bad days my mind?', and the reflections on themes from Marcus Aurelius in the 1867 sonnets 'The Better Part' and 'Worldly Place' (*Poems* 110, 526, 528).

[7] Preface to *E in C I* (1865) (*CPW* iii 287).

[8] *Empedocles on Etna* Ii 151–52 (*Poems* 163).

[9] Preface to first edition of *Poems* (1853), loc. cit. 2–3. See also John P. Farrell, ' "What you feel, I share" . . .'

[10] 'George Sand' (1877) (*CPW* viii 216–36).

[11] Letter to J. C. Shairp, 22 February 1847, *The Correspondence of Arthur Hugh Clough*, ed. Frederick L. Mulhauser (1957), i 178–9.

[12] *Trilling*, 381.

[13] *Literature and Dogma: An Essay Towards a Better Apprehension of the Bible* (1873; popular edition 1883); *God and the Bible* (1875) (*CPW* vi 140–416, vii 139–398).

[14] On 'Marguerite' and the 'Switzerland' poems see Miriam Allott, 'Arnold

and "Marguerite"—Continued', and Park Honan's reply, 'The Character of Marguerite in Arnold's *Switzerland*' (*VP* vol. 23, no. 2, summer 1985; 125–43, 145–59).

[15] 'The Better Part' (1867), beginning, 'Long fed on boundless hopes, O race of man . . .' (see note 6 above).

[16] Arnold describes Marcus Aurelius as 'wise, just, self-governed, tender, thankful, blameless,' in his essay 'Marcus Aurelius', *E in CI* (1865) (*CPW* iii 157).

[17] Letter to Lady de Rothschild, 14 October 1864 (*Letters* i 242).

[18] Letter to Clough, 1 May 1853 (*CL* 136).

[19] For a detailed account of the background to *Schools and Universities on the Continent* (1868), including Arnold's travels abroad and meetings with leading figures, see R. H. Super's commentary (*CPW* iv 344–53).

[20] 'People do not understand what a temptation there is, if you cannot bear anything not *very good*, to transfer your operations to a region where form is everything. Perfection of a kind may there be attained, or at least approached, without knocking yourself to pieces, but to attain or approach perfection in the region of thought and feeling, and to unite this with perfection of form, demands not merely an effort and a labour, but an actual tearing of oneself to pieces which one does not readily consent to (although one is sometimes forced to it) unless one can devote one's whole life to poetry.' Letter of 6 September, 1858 (*Letters* i 62–3).

[21] See Arnold's letter to Clough, 30 November 1853, 'I am glad you like the Gipsy Scholar—but what does it *do* for you? Homer *animates*—Shakespeare *animates*—in its poor way I think 'Sohrab and Rustum' *animates*—the Gipsy Scholar at best awakens a pleasing melancholy. But this is not what we want.

> The complaining millions of men
> Darken in labour and pain—

what they want is something to *animate* and *ennoble* them—not merely to add zest to their melancholy or grace to their dreams' (*CL* 146). The lines are from Arnold's own 'The Youth of Nature' ll. 51–2 (*Poems* 61).

[22] 'The spectacle of a writer striving evidently to get breast to breast with reality is always full of instruction and very invigorating . . .', letter of 20 July 1848 (*CL* 86).

[23] It is perhaps a sign of the time and its disclosures that the main title decided upon for a commemorative conference planned for the summer of 1988 (at the University of Liverpool, the city where Arnold died), should be 'Culture and its Rating at the Present Time' and that its main concerns should be non-specialist and interdisciplinary.

[24] Letter to his mother, 7 January 1863 (*Letters* i 170).

Arnold and the Movement of Mind:
The Four States of 'In Utrumque Paratus'*

NICHOLAS SHRIMPTON

Matthew Arnold the critic said many striking things about Matthew Arnold the poet. Few of them, however, have proved more memorable than the comparison which he formulated in a letter to his mother on the 5th of June, 1869:

> My poems represent, on the whole, the main movement of mind of the last quarter of a century, and thus they will probably have their day as people become conscious to themselves of what that movement of mind is, and interested in the literary productions which reflect it. It might be fairly urged that I have less poetical sentiment than Tennyson, and less intellectual vigour and abundance than Browning; yet, because I have perhaps more of a fusion of the two than either of them, and have more regularly applied that fusion to the main line of modern development, I am likely enough to have my turn, as they have had theirs.[1]

The occasion, appropriately, was the appearance of Arnold's first 'Collected Poems' (*Poems* 1869), and as a crisp summary of the salient characteristics of the major verse of the period, it is hard to better. Arnold himself, to use his own terminology, is 'adequate', a writer capable of living in 'a current of ideas' and of working in the 'world of knowledge and intelligence' of his era.[2] Unlike the English poets of the first quarter of the century, who 'did not know enough',[3] the author of 'Dover Beach', 'Stanzas from the Grande Chartreuse', and *Empedocles on Etna* registers the new thought of his age with peculiar clarity and precision.

Few critics can resist the temptation to use this suggestive self-description. R. H. Super, for example, in his book *The Time-Spirit of Matthew Arnold*, calls his first chapter 'The Main Movement of Mind', and observes, in a summary as briskly expert as Arnold's own:

> The main movement of mind—to simplify a great deal too much—

*For the texts of 1849 and 1877, with their variants, see Appendix (p. 125).

was a combination of Carlyle's analysis of the state of England,
Goethe's catholicity and disinterestedness, and Spinoza's firm
grasp of the true relation between man and the universe, of the true
essence of the Old and New Testaments.[4]

As a sketch of Arnold's chief intellectual landmarks, this is admirable,
yet like most accounts of Arnold's statement it remains in one respect
curiously incomplete. The 'movement of mind' described here seems
to be something achieved and static, a body of knowledge grasped and
incorporated into verse. Arnold's metaphor of 'movement' is, of
course, not static but dynamic, an account of change and process. We
still need, I think, to ask what Arnold meant by his own most celebrated
description of his poetry.

The poem 'In Utrumque Paratus', little discussed and never, I
think, fully understood, suggests just how much Arnold might have
meant when he spoke of 'development' and of the 'movement' of the
modern mind. It does so because it is a poem which Arnold submitted
to radical and repeated revision. Like Auden, Arnold was a poet who
would not let statements which he could no longer endorse stand in
new editions of his work. Auden's suppression of 'Spain, 1937', for
example, has a precedent in Arnold's suppression of *Empedocles on
Etna*. Similarly, Auden's rewriting of the Marxist 'Out on the lawn I
lie in bed' of 1933 into the humanist and incipiently Christian 'A
Summer Night' of 1945, has parallels in Arnold's practice. The particular ideas involved are very different, but the procedure is essentially
the same. In four successive states or versions of 'In Utrumque
Paratus', I would suggest, we see Arnold reflecting the 'movement' of
mind in his lifetime with peculiar sensitivity and sophistication.

What does not change in 'In Utrumque Paratus' is its fundamental
strategy. The title announces an intellectual double-bind. It alludes to
Aeneid ii 61, in which the Greek agent Sinon, captured by Trojans, is
faced with the two alternatives of extreme danger or certain death, and
is 'prepared in either case'.[5] The reader, like Sinon, is offered two
choices, in this case two alternative philosophical explanations of the
nature of the universe. One of these is religious, the other not. Which-
ever choice we make, however, we are to find ourselves driven to the
same inescapable conclusion. Throughout the poem's history (except,
perhaps, in what I shall call the text's second state), its argument
remains a demonstration, or an enaction in the reader's experience, of
the assertion made in ll.32–5, '. . . man . . . /Be not too proud!'
(*Poems* 46). The alternative to the traditional, humble sense of our

remote and inadequate grasp of an omniscient divine wisdom is not self-satisfaction, but rather an equally humble sense of the inadequacies of human perception.

What does change, from decade to decade, is Arnold's sense of the terms in which such an argument can be conducted. The pride involved is of a specific kind, namely the Enlightenment assertion that man can, empirically, know, explain, and understand the world. This 'proud' assumption is to be thrown into doubt, and the limits of empiricism suggested. Arnold is writing, in other words, a sceptical onslaught on scepticism, or, more precisely, on the scientific materialism which has thrown Christianity into doubt. Caught between religious and materialist explanations of the world, the reader is to find that the latter provides no more confident a sense of the independent powers of human perception than the former. Arnold's problem is to find philosophically convincing, and philosophically current, versions of the second stage of his argument—formulations which will ('adequately') persuade an educated, modern reader of the insufficiency of empiricism. The agility with which he does so is made clear by a close study of his processes of revision, and transforms our understanding of the way in which the poem functions.

Throughout the poem's history the first, religious, choice can (and does) remain unaltered. One explanation of the nature of the universe is that God made it, that it is an emanation of the divine:

> . . . in the silent mind of One all-pure,
>   At first imagined lay
> The sacred world; and by procession sure
> From those still deeps . . .
>   Took then its all-seen way (ll.1–7, *Poems* 45)

Drawing, as Kenneth Allott argued, on his reading of Plotinus in 1846,[6] Arnold first shows how matter derives (according to this theory) from spirit, and then dramatizes the process of pilgrimage by which we must strive to return to the transcendent purity which lies behind the 'coloured dream/Of life . . .' Consciousness precedes matter, but reuniting ourselves with it involves an arduous purification. Put more crudely than either Arnold or Plotinus would allow, if God (or the 'One all-pure') made the world, then man must be humble because we cannot hope to know Him (or it) fully.

Articulating on the simple pivot of a 'But', the poem then offers the alternative, materialist explanation of the universe, and of mind. The cosmos may be simply a series of chemical reactions, or atoms in motion, in which human consciousness is an accidental, belated, and unique development:

> . . . the wild unfathered mass no birth
>   In divine seats hath known;
> In the blank, echoing solitude . . . Earth . . .
>   Forms, what she forms, alone;
>
> O seeming sole to awake, thy sun-bathed head
>   Piercing the solemn cloud
> Round thy still dreaming brother-world outspread!
> O man . . .
>
> (ll.22–32, Poems 46)

Man is the sole sentient being in a world which has otherwise not developed to the stage of consciousness. Why in these circumstances should he not be proud, not assume that his mind is a sufficient and effective measure of all things?

Arnold's answer in the text printed in *The Strayed Reveller* in 1849 (though probably written as early as 1846) is, in a word, a transcendental one. He deploys a version of the Kantian argument that 'the nature of objects considered as things in themselves and without reference to the receptivity of our sensibility is quite unknown to us'.[7] Lockeian empiricists had, of course, allowed that knowledge consisted in the last resort only of 'ideas', or impressions of objects. But they also argued that those objects did indeed exist, independently of consciousness, and that they were (however imperfectly apprehended) the sole materials of our knowledge. Though the human mind does not rule the world, in the sense of bringing it into being, its generalizations from experience constitute the sole and sufficient measure of existence. Kantians believe that this theory of knowledge is no longer tenable. They, by contrast, give the human mind a 'monarch's . . . part' (1.39, *Poems* 46), insisting on the reality of an *a priori* knowledge whose conditions of perception translate sensation into consciousness by inherent laws prior to experience. In Kant's words, 'the object conforms to the nature of our faculty of intuition'.[8] But this very process of mastery cuts us off from the possibility of direct knowledge of objects considered as things in themselves without reference to the receptivity of our sensibility:

> Chief dreamer, own thy dream!
> Thy brother-world stirs at thy feet unknown,
> Who hath a monarch's hath no brother's part;
>
> (ll.37–9, *Poems* 46)

Arnold reinforces this point with the further Kantian argument that our knowledge of the self is of the same kind as our knowledge of the external world:

> . . . we must also confess, with regard to the internal sense, that by means of it we intuite ourselves only as we are internally affected by ourselves; in other words, as regards internal intuition, we cognize our own subject only as phenomenon, and not as it is in itself.[9]

Exaggerating the Kantian notion of conditioned perception into the more worrying idea of 'dream', Arnold endeavours to undermine both the empiricist world-view and the secure notion of the individual human mind on which the procedures of scientific materialism rely:

> -Oh, what a spasm shakes the dreamer's heart!
> '*I, too, but seem.*' (ll.41–2, *Poems* 47)

Either, the poem argues, God made the world (and we can't know Him), or our knowledge of the (godless) world has the imperfect status of a dream. Caught between these alternatives, *in utrumque paratus*, we are to retain the humility of the religious habit of mind, finding that scientific scepticism can itself be treated sceptically.

For a young poet interested in ideas to use transcendentalist arguments in this way was, of course, in the 1840s not surprising. Coleridge, Carlyle, and Emerson had, by 1846, made such Kantian (and post-Kantian) thought familiar to the English-speaking world. John Stuart Mill summed it up in 1840, in his 'Coleridge' essay, as 'the Germano-Coleridgian doctrine', presenting it as 'the revolt of the human mind against the philosophy of the eighteenth century' and as one of the two alternative possibilities for the 'thinking men' of his age (the other, for Mill, being a Benthamite empiricism).[10] The young Arnold clearly responded to it with excitement, an excitement registered at the time in poems such as 'Written in Emerson's Essays' and 'Morality' (with its argument for an *a priori* moral sense, and its Kantian reference to time and space as mere conditions of perception). Four decades later, in his 1885 essay on Emerson, Arnold

remembered fondly that, 'Forty years ago, when I was an under-
graduate at Oxford, voices were in the air there which haunt my
memory still.'[11] The voices are identified as those of Newman,
Carlyle, and Emerson (with Goethe indirectly heard via Carlyle's
translation of *Wilhelm Meister*). Arnold's reading lists make it clear that
between 1845 and 1847 an enthusiasm for Kantian (or neo-Kantian)
ideas derived from such 'voices' was backed up with a direct reading of
Kant.[12] Even the least sympathetic of his early reviewers was in no
doubt about the philosophical stance of 'In Utrumque Paratus'.
Charles Kingsley, though choosing for some reason to read an appeal
for humility as an expression of pride, commented in *Fraser's Magazine*
in May 1849:

> What . . . on earth do we want with à piece of obscure tran-
> scendentalism headed, *In utrumque paratus*; the moral, or we should
> rather say immorality, of which seems to be, that if there is a God,
> the author knows how to get on, and knows equally well how to get
> on if there is none?[13]

The poem, in other words, represents an application of Arnold's
gifts to 'the main line of modern development'—a use in verse of
current philosophical material. Yet after its appearance in *The Strayed
Reveller* in 1849 it disappeared for twenty years. It was not reprinted in
the editions of 1852, 1853, 1854, 1855, 1857 or (when even *Empedocles
on Etna* was allowed to return) 1867. The second of its four states is one
of absence. Why?

One possibility, of course, might be that Arnold, for formal or
aesthetic reasons, simply did not think it good enough. But, unlike
'The Hayswater Boat' which appeared in 1849 but never again, he did
reprint 'In Utrumque Paratus' in 1869, and kept it in print thereafter
for the rest of his life. It seems to me more probable that Arnold
dropped the poem from his 1852 collection because 'the movement of
mind' had made its argument no longer sustainable.

In 1840 Mill had described 'the Germano-Coleridgian doctrine' as
one of the two possible positions for the serious contemporary thinker.
But since then the doctrine had suffered some serious shocks. Mark
Pattison summarizes the process in a potted history of philosophical
fashions at Oxford in Chapter 5 of his *Memoirs*:

> When Tractarianism had made the clergy aware of their own
> strength, and high sacerdotal doctrines were openly proclaimed,

we fell off from Whately, and vague, indefinite, realistic views under the influence of Coleridge and Sir William Hamilton slowly occupied the schools. They established themselves there in a more explicit form when Mansel, a Tory leader and arch-jobber, became the logical legislator of the school, and first introduced Kant into Oxford. But the High Church party received in Newman's secession a blow which for the moment seemed fatal to their cause. Coincident with this, was the appearance of Mill's great work, and Oxford repudiated at once sacerdotal principles and Kantian logic. There was, in the language of the clerical platform, an outbreak of infidelity. For more than a quarter of this century Mill and nominalistic views reigned in the schools.[14]

Newman joined the Roman Catholic Church in 1845. Mill's *A System of Logic, Ratiocinative and Inductive* appeared in 1843. Whether or not Pattison is right to link them, and despite the inevitable over-simplification of his summary (spoken, of course, with all the bitterness of the belatedly unconverted), there does seem to have been a change of philosophical climate in the late 1840s, and Mill's book has a great deal to do with it.

The *System of Logic* is more technical, and less openly controversial, than Pattison's account might lead one to suppose. Mill himself states in his Introduction that:

> Logic is common ground on which the partisans of Hartley and of Reid, of Locke and of Kant, may meet and join hands. Particular and detached opinions of all these thinkers will no doubt occasionally be controverted . . . but the field on which their principal battles have been fought, lies beyond the boundaries of our science.[15]

Mill could, however, here be accused of being disingenuous. His very redefinition of logic as the Theory of Proof, rather than of Consistency (the science merely of 'the Formal Laws of Thought') involves an implicit challenge to the Germano-Coleridgian school and, as his subtitle suggests, he is resolutely inductive. In the words of his most recent editor, R. F. McRae, 'Mill's logic . . . is a "logic of experience" . . . its single most important thesis . . . is that all inference is from particulars to particulars'.[16] Though reasoning may proceed from the general to the particular, the general is itself simply a summary of particulars in which no *a priori* knowledge is involved:

Whiteness . . . is the name of the colour exclusively: white is a name of all things whatever having the colour; a name, not of the quality whiteness, but of every white object.[17]

In his *Autobiography* (published posthumously in 1873, but written in its 'Early Draft' in 1853–4), Mill would make the contentious nature of such assertions clear:

> The German, or *a priori* view of human knowledge, and of the knowing faculties, is likely for some time longer (though it may be hoped in a diminishing degree) to predominate among those who occupy themselves in such inquiries, both here and on the Continent. But the 'System of Logic' supplies what was much wanted, a text-book of the opposite doctrine—that which derives all knowledge from experience, and all moral and intellectual qualities principally from the direction given to the associations.[18]

Though Mill did not actually call himself an 'empiricist', reserving the term (by a fine technical distinction since abandoned) for a theory less scientific and rigorous than his own philosophy of 'Experience', he belongs very firmly to that tradition. Often closer to Bacon than to Locke in his willingness to insist that the objects of the understanding are indeed things rather than mere 'ideas' (the hypothetical causes of our sensations), he re-establishes the claims of the empirical world-view.

Arnold studied the first two books of the *System of Logic* while preparing for the Oriel fellowship examination in 1845.[19] By the 23rd of October 1850 he would be writing to Clough, 'I go to read Locke on the Conduct of the Understanding: my respect for the reason as the rock of refuge to this poor exaggerated surexcited humanity increases and increases'.[20] He was not alone. R. H. Hutton, discussing Mill's book in the *Prospective Review* in February 1850, observed:

> The prolonged silence with which his book has been received by English critics seems to imply a surrender without terms; and in fact the qualities of Mr Mill's mind are eminently calculated to impress and frighten our countrymen into silence, even when unconvinced.[21]

Whether or not Arnold remained 'unconvinced', he certainly fell silent. Responding to a 'movement of mind', recognizing, as less intellectual poets might not, that the transcendental (or 'Germano-Coleridgian')

prong of the argument of 'In Utrumque Paratus' would no longer
serve, he duly dropped the poem.

From 1852 to 1868 it remains absent from successive reprintings of
his poetry. This absence did not, however, exempt Arnold from attacks
on his work as benightedly Germano-Coleridgian. James Fitzjames
Stephen, reviewing 'The Function of Criticism at the Present Time' in
the *Saturday Review* on 3 December 1864, remarked that 'Mr Arnold's
whole essay assumes the truth of the transcendental theory of philosophy . . . Mr Arnold surely cannot be ignorant of the fact that, from
the days of Hobbes and Locke to those of Mr Mill and Mr Bain, the
most influential of English thinkers have utterly denied the truth of
transcendentalism, and have constantly affirmed that all knowledge is
based on experience and sensation . . .'.[22] We know that Arnold was
stung by this criticism because he replied to it, publicly and at length:

> About a year ago the *Saturday Review* published an article which
> gave me, as its articles often do give me, much food for reflection
> . . . It appears that I assume the truth of the transcendental system
> of philosophy, and then lecture my wiser countrymen because they
> will not join me in recognising as eternal truths a set of platitudes
> which may be proved to be false. 'Now there is in England a school
> of philosophy which thoroughly understands, and, on theoretical
> grounds, deliberately rejects, the philosophical theory which Mr
> Arnold accuses the English nation of neglecting; and the practical
> efforts of the English people, especially their practical efforts in the
> way of criticism, are for the most part strictly in accordance with the
> principles of that philosophy.'
> I do not quite know what to say about the transcendental system
> of philosophy, for I am a mere dabbler in these great matters, and
> to grasp and hold a system of philosophy is a feat much beyond my
> strength; but I certainly did talk about British Philistines . . . when
> they are doing just what the wisest men in the country have settled
> to be quite right . . .[23]

The affected ignorance of philosophy is, of course, a debating trick.
When 'The Function of Criticism at the Present Time' was first
reprinted in book form (in *Essays in Criticism* 1865), Arnold added a
long footnote (subsequently deleted) in which he took pains to identify
the precise philosophical stance of his hostile reviewer:

> I have no doubt my reviewer, with his scientific powers, can easily
> invent some beautiful formula to make us appear to be doing this

[sc. selling army commissions] on the purest philosophical principles; the principles of Hobbes, Locke, Bentham, Mr Mill, Mr
Bain, and himself, their worthy disciple.[24]

And in a passage present in the first edition of the preface to *Essays in
Criticism*, but similarly deleted in editions later than 1865, Arnold
addresses himself directly to the dispute between the two conflicting
theories of perception, in terms which, incidentally, make it clear that
he assumes Mill's inductive logic to be the contemporary norm:

> . . . I have never been able to hit it off happily with the logicians,
> and it would be mere affectation in me to give myself the airs of
> doing so. They imagine truth something to be proved, I something
> to be seen; they something to be manufactured, I as something to
> be found. I have a profound respect for intuitions, and a very
> lukewarm respect for the elaborate machine-work of my friends the
> logicians. I have always thought that all which was worth much in
> this elaborate machine-work of theirs came from an intuition, to
> which they gave a grand name of their own. How did they come by
> this intuition? Ah! if they could tell us that.[25]

But if the ignorance of philosophy was an affectation, so, I suspect,
was Arnold's ability to carelessly shrug off the attack. A poet who
prides himself on his consciousness of 'the main line of modern development' is likely to be sensitive to suggestions that he is out of touch
with contemporary philosophical opinion. So in 1869, when at the
invitation of his new publisher he assembles a collected edition of his
verse, he covers his tracks. He reprints his most outspokenly transcendental poem, but rewrites it to remove the transcendentalism.[26]

The 'In Utrumque Paratus' of 1869 (its third state) is still a
recommendation of humility, and still an attack on empiricism. But
the Kantian theory of lines 36–42 has entirely disappeared. Sympathetic though Arnold may still find it, he knows that in the contemporary climate of opinion it will not serve as a clinching argument.
Instead he draws on a more recent product of the movement of mind,
the evolutionary ideas which had been given such controversial
reinforcement by the publication of Darwin's *On the Origin of Species* in
1859:

> Thy native world stirs at thy feet unknown,
>   Yet there thy secret lies!
> Out of this stuff, these forces, thou art grown,

And proud self-severance from them were disease.
O scan thy native world with pious eyes!
High as thy life be risen, 'tis from these,
    And these, too, rise.

(ll.36–42n, *Poems* 46)

Once again the suggestion is that we must approach the world with 'pious eyes', rather than the self-confidence of the scientific material-ist. But the reason supplied is no longer a philosophical claim about the nature of perception. Rather, Arnold argues that the rest of matter is evolving towards the human condition of consciousness, with the result that we are not unique. It also follows, by implication at least, that empirical observation is limited because it is examining an evolving rather than a static world. If matter is changing as we look at it, then, as before, we cannot hope fully to know it.

This is an ingenious revision, and one which shows a remarkable ability (appropriate perhaps in a poet using Darwinian argument) to adapt to a changing intellectual climate. Arnold's letter to his mother, in which he bases his achievement as a poet on his representation of 'the main movement of mind of the last quarter of a century' and his regular application of his powers to 'the main line of modern develop-ment', was written on the 5th of June 1869 to announce the appear-ance of the very volume in which this revision appears ('My book was out yesterday').[27] It is hard to resist the feeling that Arnold had such adaptations as this particularly in mind when he used his famous phrase.

But the most striking alteration of 'In Utrumque Paratus' was, in fact, still to come. In 1877 Arnold published a second collected edition of his poems, rearranged and enlarged. Once again 'In Utrumque Paratus' was revised, entering its fourth and final state. But that fourth state is identical with the first state. In the late 1870s Arnold restores his transcendental argument.

The few commentators who have attempted to explain this change have tended to suggest a simple dissatisfaction with the text of 1869. Tinker and Lowry argue that the notion of the world of matter's evolu-tion into consciousness 'may have seemed to the poet too startling an innovation to retain'.[28] Kenneth Allott remarks that 'The apparent connection here with topical Victorian ideas of evolution seems to have irked Arnold' (*Poems* 47). In light of the previous history of the poem's development, I would suggest that we can see a more signifi-cant, and more positive, process here. Between 1869 and 1877 the intellectual climate has changed once again, and Arnold is aware of it.

Mark Pattison, who supplied so convenient a sketch of the previous shift in philosophical fashion, is once again helpful. The passage from his *Memoirs* quoted above speaks of a 'quarter of a century' in which 'Mill and nominalistic views reigned'. This takes us to 1870, and Pattison explains what, in his view, then occurred:

> But gradually the clerical party rallied their forces, and since the Franco-German war have been advancing upon us with rapid strides. This fresh invasion of sacerdotalism has been accompanied by a renewed attempt to accredit an *a priori* logic, though in a less cumbrous form than the Kantian, bristling as that does with postulates and assumptions—ideas of the reason, ideas of the understanding, the two *Anschauungsformen*, and all the other *Begriffsdichtungen* with which the Kantian loves to decorate his imaginative chamber. What is curious is that this new *a priori* metaphysic, whoever gave it shape in Germany, was imported into Oxford by a staunch Liberal, the late Professor Green.[29]

What Pattison is describing is the idealist revival, the work of the so-called English Neo-Hegelians. Since the mid-1860s a rediscovery of idealist philosophy had been under way. This process is often attributed to the belated translation into English of Hegel: James Hutchison Stirling's *The Secret of Hegel* (which includes a translation of the first part of the *Wissenschaft der Logik*) was published in 1865; Wallace's *The Logic of Hegel* (a translation, with commentary, of the 'Lesser Logic' from Hegel's *Encyclopaedia of the Philosophical Sciences*) followed in 1874. But this new school of thought also had other sources. Joseph Henry Green, the disciple charged in Coleridge's will with the responsibility for systematizing his philosophy, died in 1863, leaving the manuscript of *Spiritual Philosophy: founded on the teaching of the late Samuel Taylor Coleridge*. The book appeared two years later. Equally important, in the view of some historians of philosophy, was the publication of Benjamin Jowett's translation of *The Dialogues of Plato* (1871). Platonic, Coleridgian, and Hegelian influences combined to usher in a new phase of English thought.

Much of that thought consisted of an attack on empiricism. The dominating figures of Pattison's 'quarter of a century' of 'Mill and nominalistic views' had been, apart from Mill himself, scientific thinkers like Herbert Spencer (whose *First Principles* appeared in 1862), T. H. Huxley, John Tyndall, and W. K. Clifford. Now a younger generation of philosophers set out to undermine their influence. One route to the achievement of this aim was by the re-assertion of Hume's development of the sceptical implications of Locke. T. H. Green's best-known works appeared only after his death in 1882. But in 1874 he published an edition of Hume's *Treatise of Human Nature*, and made its controversial purpose clear in his Introduction:

> Our business . . . has not been to moralise, but to show that the philosophy based on the abstraction of feeling, in regard to morals no less than to nature, was with Hume played out, and that the next step forward in speculation could only be an effort to re-think the process of nature and human action from its true beginning in thought. If this object has been in any way attained, so that the attention of Englishmen 'under five-and-twenty' may be diverted from the anachronistic systems hitherto prevalent among us to the study of Kant and Hegel, an irksome labour will not have been in vain.[30]

Mill's inductive logic is suddenly 'anachronistic'; Kantian views are once again tenable. T. H. Green (like Arnold, a product of Rugby and Balliol) became Whyte's Professor of Moral Philosophy at Oxford in 1878. Arnold was certainly aware of Green's work by the end of 1877, since he transcribes two passages from his article 'Mr Herbert Spencer and Mr G. H. Lewes; Their Application of the Doctrine of Evolution to Thought' (printed in the *Contemporary Review*, December 1877) into his 1877 notebook:

> The primary question of metaphysics: *How is knowledge possible?*

> 'Kant set himself to ascertain what the relations are which are necessary to constitute any intelligent experience', or (which is the same) 'any knowable world'. Green on H. Spencer.[31]

Though we here seem very close indeed to the concerns of 'In Utrumque Paratus', the notes must post-date Arnold's decision to revise the poem (*Poems* 1877 had been published in the summer, and noticed by the *Spectator* on 1 July). But Arnold had been making notes on Hegel in his 1874 notebook,[32] and on Coleridge in 1866.[33] Indeed, his objection to the inductive logicians in the deleted passage in the preface to *Essays in Criticism* in 1865 ('I have always thought that all which was worth much in this elaborate machine-work of theirs came from an intuition')[34] might be said to have anticipated an argument which the new idealists would strive, more rigorously, to demonstrate.

Though the full-scale riposte to Mill's *A System of Logic* would not appear until 1883 (F. H. Bradley's *Principles of Logic*), Neo-Hegelian or Neo-Kantian theory was well established by 1877. Even the hostile Mark Pattison allowed that it might have its uses:

> As a chastisement for the egoism and the ignorant adoption of fashionable freethinking, which now characterises young Oxford, it may do good service if it merely restore to us the lost virtues of humility, reverence, and recognition of a power beyond ourselves. The galvanised Kantism, which seems to be coming into esteem, will lead to a re-examination of the old problem of thought, and thus a reasoned conviction may arise to take the place of a lazy and thoughtless acquiescence in the opinions of the fashionable periodicals.[35]

In such circumstances Matthew Arnold was fully entitled to feel that the original, Kantian ending of his poem would once again carry the force which the double-bind structure of his argument required. He duly restored it. The poem's final state is the same as its original state, not for reasons of negligence or indifference, but because the 'movement of mind', and a scrupulous attention to the 'main line of modern development', required it to be so. 'In Utrumque Paratus' is an early poem, and a minor one. It none the less demonstrates, with peculiar clarity, three important things. One is the instability of text. Another is the extreme sensitivity of text to context (read in the wrong decade, the poem, as Arnold knows, would fail to function). And the third is just how much is really involved in being, seriously, a poet of ideas.

Notes

[1] *Letters* ii 9.

[2] 'On the Modern Element in Literature' (14 November 1857), *CPW* i 29, and 'The Function of Criticism at the Present Time' (November 1864), *E in C I* (*CPW* iii 263).

[3] 'The Function of Criticism at the Present Time', *CPW* iii 262.

[4] R. H. Super, *The Time Spirit of Matthew Arnold* (1970), 29.

[5] See Virgil, *Aeneid* 2, 61–2:

. . . fidens animi atque in utrumque paratus,
seu versare dolos seu certae occumbere morti.

Deconstructive readers will note that one of the alternatives in this allusion is actually the telling of a lie. Sinon is a Greek double-agent, who has deliberately allowed himself to be captured by the Trojans (posing as a deserter) in order to persuade them to accept the Horse. He is prepared either 'to spin his web of lies' (versare dolos) or to be killed on the spot. Arnold may also be thinking of Sinon's subsequent experience in Troy, where he presents himself as being, simultaneously, rejected by the Greeks and suspected by the Trojans.

[6] See K. Allott, 'Matthew Arnold's Reading-Lists in Three Early Diaries', in *Victorian Studies* 2 (March 1959), 262 and *Poems* 44.

[7] Kant, *Critique of Pure Reason*, transl. Meiklejohn (Everyman, 1950), 54.

[8] Ibid., 12.

[9] Ibid., 107.

[10] J. S. Mill, 'Coleridge', *London & Westminster Review* (March 1840); *Collected Works of John Stuart Mill* (Toronto, 1969), 125; and 'Bentham', *London & Westminster Review* (August 1838), ibid., 77.

[11] 'Emerson' (first delivered as a lecture, 1 December 1883), *Discourses in America* (1885) (*CPW* x 165).

[12] See K. Allott, 'Matthew Arnold's Reading-Lists in Three Early Diaries', loc. cit. 258, 263.

[13] Charles Kingsley, unsigned review, *Fraser's Magazine* xxix (May 1849), reprinted *Dawson* (1973), 43.

[14] Mark Pattison, *Memoirs* (1885), 166.

[15] J. S. Mill, *A System of Logic, Ratiocinative and Inductive* (1843); *Works* ed. cit. vii (1974), 14.

[16] Ibid., xxviii.

[17] Ibid., 30.

[18] J. S. Mill, *Autobiography* (1873), *Works* ed. cit. i (1961), 233.

[19] See K. Allott, 'Matthew Arnold's Reading-Lists . . .', loc. cit. 258.

[20] *CL* 116; see Kenneth Allott on this letter, 'Between 1845 and 1850 I think it is possible to trace Arnold's growing impatience with German idealism . . .', 'Matthew Arnold's Reading-Lists . . .', loc. cit. 261n.

[21] R. H. Hutton, 'Mill and Whewell on the Logic of Induction', *Prospective Review* vi (February 1850), quoted Mill's *Works* ed. cit. vii (1974), lxxxii.

[22] James Fitzjames Stephen, 'Mr. Matthew Arnold and his Countrymen', *Saturday Review* xviii (3 December 1864), cited *CPW* v 363.

[23] 'My Countrymen', *Cornhill Magazine* (February 1866); *Friendship's Garland* (*CPW* v 3–4). cp. 'Disconcerting the Reader . . .' (p. 35).

[24] 'The Function of Criticism at the Present Time', *E in C1* 1865 (only), (*CPW* iii 531).

25 Preface to *E in C 1* 1865 (only) (*CPW* iii 535-6).

26 Swinburne had reminded the reading public of the poem's existence when reviewing Arnold's *New Poems* (1867). He quoted 11.15-21, commenting, 'These noble verses of another poem clipped from Mr. Arnold's first book, and left hanging in fragments about one's memory—I here make my protest against its excision—may serve as types of the later, the more immediate and elaborate discourse of thought . . .', *Fortnightly Review* ns 2 (October 1867); *Dawson*, 165. When Swinburne reprinted his review in *Essays & Studies* (1875) he added the footnote, 'It has since been replaced, with the final stanza wholly rewritten. For its recovery I believe that I may take some credit to myself, and claim in consequence some thanks from all serious students of contemporary poetry', *The Bonchurch Edition of the Complete Works of Algernon Charles Swinburne* (1925-7), 5, 66.

27 *Letters* ii 9.

28 *Commentary* 55.

29 Mark Pattison, *Memoirs* (1885), 166-7.

30 T. H. Green, *Introduction to the Moral Part of Hume's 'Treatise of Human Nature'* (1874) in *Works of Thomas Henry Green*, ed. R. L. Nettleship (1885), 1, 371.

31 *Note-books* 284.

32 Ibid., 215.

33 Ibid., 40.

34 Preface to *E in C I* 1865 (only) (*CPW* iii 535-6).

35 Mark Pattison, *Memoirs* (1885), 243.

Disconcerting the Reader: Friendship's Garland *and the True Voices of* 'Mr. Arnold'

BRIAN NELLIST

Friendship's Garland (1871) looks at first a changeling among Arnold's legitimate progeny, a work of fiction among words of truth, a toy on the library floor. Arnold's prose works characteristically announce their subjects in their titles and, however surprisingly 'vivacious', to use one of his own words, the discussion, those subjects are learned or large or often both. But what are we to make of a title which indicates a commemorative volume for a fictional Prussian savant—the subject of actual letters, written as long as five years before—to the actual *Pall Mall Gazette*, by an equally fictional 'Matthew Arnold'? Why in this work does Arnold so gleefully disguise his voice, presenting himself as trapped between sound patriotic instincts and awed submission to the strident criticisms of his mentor, a kind of Victorian Gulliver? This is a parody invented out of contemporary criticism of Arnold, defensive about his attachment to England but too easily impressed by Germanic earnestness or French wit. Obviously, many of what we take to be the true Arnold's opinions, expressed apparently without irony elsewhere, are here attributed to Arminius Von Thunder-ten-Tronckh. Yet the unpolemical flow of Arnold's persuasions elsewhere becomes here a ferocious knock-down style, a kind of ventriloquist Carlyle: 'You peck at the mere outside of problems: you have not got your mind at work upon them; you fancy they will solve themselves without mind, if only you keep making bottles, and letting everyone do what is right in his own eyes, and congratulating yourselves at the top of your voices on your own success'.[1] The ironical displacement is confirmed by the narrative: Arminius's concern for his Candidean genealogy, his image as a blond, pipe-smoking giant who leaves bad debts wherever he goes. In its serious playfulness, its refusal to let the reader settle on safe ground, its interest in contrasted styles of discussion, this is the nearest thing the age produces to Scriblerian writing.

Swift and Voltaire were, among the moderns, the prose writers Arnold admired[2], and the adroitness of their ironies is not only useful to remember in reading the *Garland* but instructive to the reader of Arnold generally. The temptation in reading this work is to unscramble its codes and decipher the various utterances that belong to Arnold the historian of post-Napoleonic Europe, Arnold on Ireland, Arnold on education, even Arnold on the phenomenology of text. *Friendship's Garland* might be more use to us, however, if it were more centrally placed and so allowed us to hear, through its magnification of them, the variations and shifts of voice throughout Arnold's work. The work persuades us that even more important than the several issues discussed is the temper of mind with which they should all be addressed, which is in the end an inherent part of style. Arnold's style is seen most completely in *Friendship's Garland* itself. Literature brings into being the minds that read it. The *Garland* is a heuristic process for readers who conceive the world in Acts of Parliament. The refusal to be categorical, the faculty of slipping easily from one idea to another, to keep coming upon the same facts by different routes, all put the reader inevitably in a position which both confirms and yet contradicts the criticisms of the English styles of thought the work is offering. *Friendship's Garland* puts in the foreground of our response to Arnold a style of thinking which claims the delicacy of Newman's habit of mind, while ironically evading Newman's language of distinctions and logic that leads inevitably in the direction of doctrine.

The art of secular (as distinct from theological) complexity is to hold separate terms of thought always in parentheses, as with the distinct voices of *Friendship's Garland*, without dissolving the brackets. Though he never again uses the particular method employed in this work, its inherent suspensions of conclusion are apparent throughout Arnold's prose. In an instance as notable as the 'Hebraism and Hellenism' chapter of *Culture and Anarchy*, one could also ask where does its centre lie, and then discover that the question has been wrongly formulated— that it is not a subject for critical debate, but for observing a subtle rallying of the categorical reader's desire to ask such a question. Does the analysis exist for the sake of the lucid social psychology, which first provides the context for the terms; for the epitome of European history, which expresses their dialectic; or for the final, pungent metaphor that Victorian society, intent as it was on discovering the sources of the Nile, has after all been following the wrong stream? Taken separately, the sections of Arnold's analysis may seem too slight to prove his case, yet the terms, Hebrew and Hellenic, cannot be dislodged from the memory, and the convergence of idea, argument, and image threatens, mocks, cajoles the reader without letting the mind settle on a single centre, finally leaving him with the anxieties that conclude the chapter. In the penultimate paragraph, just when the reader is brought to the possibility of being bypassed by history, Arnold will write of English culture:

> Eminently Indo-European by its *humour*, by the power it shows, through this gift, of imaginatively acknowledging the multiform aspects of the problem of life, and of thus getting itself unfixed from its own over-certainty, of smiling at its own over-tenacity, our race has yet (and a great part of its strength lies here) in matters of practical life and moral conduct, a strong share of the assuredness, the tenacity, the intensity of the Hebrews.[3]

The long qualification at the start of the sentence almost takes over the centre of its meaning before we see what is being qualified, and the critical term, Hebraism, is described with such respect that out of context is sounds like praise. The reader scarcely knows whether to be reassured or rebuked or which part of the sentence offers either. The sentence, like the chapter and the book itself, takes over the role that Arnold, significantly if we keep *Friendship's Garland* in mind, attributes to humour, of 'acknowledging the multiform aspects of the problem'. To read the sentence creates inevitably in the reader's mind the delicate sense of 'getting itself unfixed from its own over-certainty'. Thinking is undoubtedly happening in such a sentence, for example in that parenthetic and pregnant suggestion that English comedy originates in English seriousness ('over-tenacity'). But even more than the separable ideas, it is the process of thought, the movement of the mind, which holds the reader's attention.

It is this combination of ringing aphorism or definitive term, 'Hebraism', with the elusiveness of the sustained style that constitutes in Arnold a kind of habitual irony. Irony is rarely used consistently by the Victorian writer, compared with eighteenth-century practice, at least, presumably because in irony we as listeners are put at a disadvantage, and the nineteenth-century writer did not want to risk that loss of trust in his audience. Certainly Frederick Harrison represents a recognizable response to Arnold's process of thought:

> If he cannnot range himself under any of the known schemes, if he be neither intuitionist, experimentalist, or eclectic, if he inclines neither to authority nor to freedom, neither to revelation, nor to scepticism, nor to any of the ways of thinking that lie between any

of these extremes—then he must have a brand-new, self-originated, dominant scheme of his own.[4]

It is I suppose possible to have a sneaking sympathy with Harrison here, while at the same time seeing in this cacophony of alternative 'systems' why Arnold's preference might be for 'silence, stealth, and cunning', like Stephen Daedalus. In *Friendship's Garland* each of the voices seems to point beyond itself by its simplicity, yet also to exist to obstruct the other voices and their rival simplifications. Ultimately, the work advocates a critical silence.

This variety of voice—for example, the comfortable words from *Culture and Anarchy* that suddenly turn critical—seems to relate to a constant in Arnold's work (one thinks of the very distinct tone of the letters to Clough, unpredictable from the Russell collection)[5], as much in the poetry as in the prose works. I am thinking here not so much of the dramatic poems but rather of the sudden changes of direction in works not thought of as dramatic. Change of tone or direction seems not as in the prose directed to specific ends, but rather to overtake the poetry, to thrust itself upon the poet's imagination. His verse scarcely seems to offer a debate which could be resolved, as in Tennyson's 'The Two Voices' or, with the price increasingly high, *In Memoriam* and *Maud* and *The Idylls*. In 'The Buried Life' the gravely analytical style is displaced finally by an image that glimpses an inner landscape; landscape can scarcely enter into debate with the severe analysis of our waking state in the major part of the poem. In 'A Summer Night' and 'Dover Beach', the reversions into image work to contrasted ends of promise and dismay. In 'Sohrab and Rustum' the interruption of the rather stretched, understated blank verse by the lyric similes is too insistent to be a simple management of the Homeric style. The separation between the constricting human world of father and son who always miss one another through misapprehensions of speech, and the unspeaking but resilient world of the lesser creation, is typical of Arnold's ironies, though also an extension of Homer. But the strength of the poem lies in its honest willingness to let lyrical desire so break into the high elegy, as though in the act of writing the poem Arnold is overtaken by a desire to resolve the division, simply resulting in a reinforcement of the split. Hence whether the final image of the Aral Sea is catharsis or ironic resignation, whether it belongs with elegy or lyric, we cannot tell, and words that sound like lyric success, 'luminous home', 'bright and tranquil', 'Emerge and shine', become in their human context the completion of death and the clarity of the legend which embalms Sohrab and Rustum in the poem itself.

In 'The Scholar-Gipsy' the landscape also functions as voice, speaking for the absent and elusive gipsy himself, of course, but through him for the memory of a lost and cherished youth in the poet, a voice that upbraids elegiacally the inelastic tones of ravaged maturity. Yet two entirely contrasted understandings of youth and age draw the poem apart as much as 'Sohrab and Rustum'. In one, youth can afford to wait, idly its enemies would say, for the 'spark from heaven', so that those who work as they must in the world find him inactive, or lethargic even amid their pleasures; the shepherds entering the inn 'Had found him seated at their entering' (l. 60), the student riders find him in a punt 'leaning backward in a pensive dream' (l. 77), maidens dancing see him 'roam' but never hear him speak (l. 90), and the hay-makers going to bathe

> Have often passed thee near
> *Sitting* upon the river bank o'ergrown (ll. 96–7; my italics)

If even the well-earned leisure of the happy and uncomplicated is too active for the gipsy, no wonder educated maturity, rat-racing after its dubious objectives, never catches a glimpse of him. Yet the gipsy's immobility is credited also with a vitality denied to modern man who, from this point of view, becomes a low-spirited, and in his turn, immobilized maturity; we 'Who hesitate and falter life away' (l. 178) or the best of us who 'takes dejectedly/His *seat* upon the intellectual throne' (ll. 183–4; my italics). This is not to suggest that there is simply an unnoticed or unadopted contradiction in the poem, but rather that different manifestations and modes of energy and stillness, of the expressed and the unexpressed, remain in the poem without an adjudicating authority to sort them out. What might have been a dispute is allowed to remain as a series of perspectives or unspoken questions.

As at the end of 'Sohrab and Rustum', so here the closing image which seems to alter the direction of the poem is really responding to its internal dilemmas. With the Tyrian trader, landscape changes to seascape, and this arena now belongs to the new man, not to the gipsy. It is the mature voices who become the young Greeks and gain light hearts, and the gipsy who now grows grave and by comparison old. However the shift of identity is explained, it always remains, in my experience, to trouble the reader who persists in trying to recall the latest exposition, convincing while it was read, of a contradiction that remains obdurately resisting explanation. Yet of two things we are sure every time we read the lines: a power, which makes them among the always remembered passages of Arnold, and a sense of confidence in them that, though unforeseen, does alter the poem's perspective. In place of contrasted kinds of inability to act, in the body of the poem, we now find contrasted images of adventure. In place of the elegy over youth, the last two stanzas extend the confines of the individual life by alluding to the inevitable and reconciling changes of history; after the Phoenicians, the Greeks. Within this sudden shift of confidence, further ironies spring; it is the apparently superannuated Tyrian, the man with the 'ancient home' as against the 'young' masters of the wave, who becomes the explorer, pushing on 'To where the Atlantic raves/Outside the western straits' (ll.246-7). The seemingly obsolete figure is actually a messenger to our Oceanic culture and the 'dark Iberians'.

This sudden intrusion of a different voice, this dialogue of articulate grieving with mute and complex intimation, is typical of Arnold's poetry, but carries over always and importantly into the prose writing. The poetry is frankly rhapsodic, and advisedly so; in the rather loose organization, words can happen in ways the reader can never quite predict. To read the poems is to enter a space where the *donnée* can occur, where the unexpected voice may speak. Similarly, the prose works are not, compared with the work of Carlyle, or Mill, or even Ruskin in the pamphlets, closely organized. They were written often periodically, and in the spaces between other men's arguments. But the very openness they provide allows room for the same shifts of tone we notice in the poems to occur more freely than if Arnold were to depend on the primacy of argument. The play of voices is wider than in the poems, called into being as counter-echoes to the contemporary alternatives that beset Arnold's ears. Amidst the language of blue-books, of political economy and its enemies, of the specialized treatise, Arnold cultivates a casualness, a deceptive slightness of utterance, that counters the raging voices with an irony of quietness, lowering the constant *fortissimo* of argument to the point where even that manner could serve as an apologetic irony; 'My debility in high speculation is well known'.[6] Inherent in the manner is the function of aphorism, the form he admired in Joubert and Bp Wilson; he converted Emerson on his home ground from transcendental philosopher to the creator of sharp sayings. If, to the modern critic, the apparatus sometimes seems unnervingly slight and the famous phrases—'to see life steady and to see it whole', 'sweetness and light', 'Hebraism and Hellenism',

'Barbarian and Philistine'—too simple for what they attempt, we might start by recollecting in the letters his impish delight in having created slogans which—as Disraeli admiringly acknowledged—can enter that language of power, the conversation of the world. The slightness makes them memorable, and once lodged they expand in the mind of the user. They are polished stones for the Schumannesque *Davidsbundler* in their march on the Philistines. Surrounded by voices, hot with the wrong kind of earnestness, over-specialized, anti-literary, he uses literature's own weapons of metaphor and irony to formulate an attack more resented, in a way more powerful, than Ruskin's frontal assault.

The elusive interplay of voices is seen even in a comparatively late work such as *God and the Bible* (1875). If he starts the book with a critique of stultified orthodoxy, it might seem as though the Liberals with their armoury of textual criticism, gleaming from the most modern German factories, would be natural allies, yet he springs round on them also, as though one enemy were not enough, and then deliberately apologizes for the poverty of his own armaments:

> . . . we sometimes flatter ourselves that we may be of use by the very absence of all scientific pretension, because we are thus obliged to treat great questions in such a simple way that any one can follow us, while the way, at the same time, may possibly be quite right after all, only overlooked by more ingenious people because it is so very simple.[7]

The delicacy with which respect ('ingenious people') is used as a mode of aggression, and disability ('such a simple way') becomes strength, and from the start self-deprecation ('we sometimes flatter ourselves') becomes defiance ('we may be of use'), replaces the argument his opponents would want to hear with ironical play, and submits itself for judgement to unprejudiced intelligence as against professional expertise.

The Christ who emerges from the final chapters of *God and the Bible* is an Arnoldian culture hero, the author himself of elusive apothegms misunderstood by the professional experts of his day, the apostles and the redactors of the Gospels. Since the whole direction of Arnold's discussion is to restore to metaphor the language of the Sacred Text, a language rendered literal over centuries of misinterpretation, the work is clearly a serious unity. Conclusion and opening assumptions agree. It is a unity of accretion, however, of reiteration and circularity rather than of linear argument. Its method is that of literary criticism, a recognition in Scripture of the moments that 'make for life', an interpretation of half-concealed meanings. Above all it involves a recognition, in a work that proceeds by the same method as it identifies in the Bible, of utterance as a kind of secrecy, of gnomic moments within an ironically lucid texture, implying what we rarely actually see. It is not that the book is not clear in its preferences, or that it is dismissably slight in its apparatus of thought and research (though it is always apologizing that it *is*) or that it is not offered as a view necessary to the salvation of the times, but that all these things of substance are discussed in a tone mockingly elusive, cunningly slight in terms of the style of theological enquiry expected by the reader of 1874. It is valiantly under-equipped. Arnold will always start with a claim which looks reductive: 'Religion is, we say, morality touched with emotion.' This is another of his mnemonic maxims, but he then understands his own saying in a way that deepens and undercuts the objections of both Liberalism and orthodoxy: 'It declares itself by the accent and power with which its utterances are made'.[8] The delicate authority of a faith grounded in supposition, persuasion, and recognition, on literary values in fact, is gradually established in the reader's mind as against both the literal categories of tradition and the purely fictive dismissals of form criticism. The slight voice turns out to have been tough all along.

This delicate process is seen with unique clarity, I believe, in *Friendship's Garland*, which stands between the voices that speak almost involuntarily in the poetry and the more directed use of voice in the discursive prose. If he never writes again as he did in *Friendship's Garland*, that is because, maybe, he never again needs to be so overt in discovering the use and value of this drama of voices.

The word round which *Friendship's Garland* turns, which by its variety of implications and its critical function works like an aphorism in other prose works, is *geist*. The German language and German history, the references to Stein's reforms, for example, offer Arnold a standard of alienation from merely English usage. *Geist* is a voice from another cultural centre which forces the surrounding English words and assumptions to come to terms with it; its semantic range—intelligence, spirit, courage, flair—represents a composite challenge to the varied obsessions and inanities Arnold attacks. In his letters he delights in this kind of discovery of the word of power: 'My letter on Geist has been a great success and I hear of it wherever I go'. So later, he will write, 'I hope you laughed over the *Barbarians*', or with still more pleasure, 'I am struck to find what hold among these younger men what I write has taken; I should think I heard the word *Philistines* used at least a hundred times during dinner, and *Barbarians* very often'.[9] Later he will ironically mock this verbal vitality, calling it, 'a frippery of phrases about sweetness and light, seeing things as they really are, . . . which never had very much solid meaning and has now quite lost the gloss and charm of novelty'.[10] Arminius, the major speaker of the *Garland*, by and large sticks to Arnold's first definition: 'In Berlin we oppose "Geist"—*intelligence* as you or the French might say,—to "Ungeist" '.[11] But the composition itself includes what escapes the rather solemn mind of Arminius: the wit and spiritedness that is also the meaning of the word.

The purpose of the wit is to so transform the conflict of words by which Arnold is surrounded—the varied public issues from popular journalism to Coles's Truss Manufactory, from Irish land reform to quarrels in the local tripe shop—that they all, real and imaginary, become instances of *ungeist*. The central issue becomes one of style, then, and the collective lack of insight that governs the national life at all levels is to be countered not by argument but by wit. Writing to his mother about Letter v, on Baron Stein's reforms in Prussia over fifty years before, he apologizes to her for his levity:

> The fact is, it is the one way in which in this country many things that have to be said can be said so as to reach those who read them. I like to think the *Star*, in order to get the benefit of the irony on landlordism, has to digest the irony on 'dissentism'.[12]

There is a good-humoured aggressiveness in that 'has to digest', in the baiting of the literary trap.

The separate non-Arminian voices in the work, each apparently simple—the Young Lion of the Press, Mr Bottles and Lord Lumpington, Philistine and Barbarian, and the Reverend Mr Hittall—who help to fictionalize the supporters of Bright and Lowe and Cobden and Palmerston, whose names also enter the work, create between them a complex of ideas, a space for thought to happen in. Unlike his other prose works, the *Garland* has the assistance of narrative, not unlike a sketch by Thackeray, involving characters who lead safe and parochial English lives and continue their debates about the 'Deceased Sister's Marriage Bill' while the great issues of Europe claim the life of Arminius. It is not this or that controversy that the work addresses; it suggests an awareness which would transform the style of controversy collectively, a sense of European movements since Napoleon and of a continent stretching from St. Petersburg to the Atlantic. Irony lies in the narrative juxtapositions, then, as well as in the style. How the work is written is the major part of what it is about: 'the one way in which many things that have to be said *can* be said'.

Arminius, earnest, downright, honest as he is in his fierceness, still differs from the viewpoint maintained by the total work, still has something of the 'moral desperado' of Arnold's Carlyle about him. The narrative partly pushes him into irony in a way that Arnold could not know when he conceived the character. For a prophet in tune with the stream of tendency, attributing Prussia's victory over Austria to 'Geist', it is unfortunate for him to die before the walls of Paris, subjected to a footnote of unwitting revenge from the bland 'Matthew Arnold', apparently in agreement with the egregious Bottles: ' "Ungeist in uniform", as Mr Bottles observes to me, has just given a pretty good account of the "Geist" in French democracy . . . Perhaps Arminius was taken away from the evil to come!'[13] In the complex style of the book, Arnold uses the turn of events between writing the first letter in 1866 and publication in book form in 1871 to turn his own term against its supposed author, but also to show it being used by a complacently stupid mind like Bottles. 'Geist' for the reader involves an appreciation of it, but less confidence in the end than Arminius has that history respects it. Elegy is an important part of the book, though not of the original letters. Arnold's distress hides itself inside the many layers of irony as the whole book becomes retrospectively an epitaph for the spirit of Frankfurt liberalism. Had Arminius survived 1870 he might have gone into exile with the Schlegels and turned up as a minor reference in E. M. Forster's *Howard's End*.

Of course, Arminius speaks for a good many of Arnold's ideas. He is made the author of those critical opinions of England first published in the essay 'My Countrymen' (1865), reprinted, with mocking footnotes tracing Arminius's voice in the work, added to the *Pall Mall* letters, and so made to compose the *Garland*. He defends middle-class schooling, pleads for imagination and generosity in the government's response to Ireland, admires Burke's England, like Arnold, but, also like Arnold, thinks the national situation has changed since Burke, and he criticizes freedom of speech as a sufficient end in itself. Yet the tone of his own voice remains wrong, argumentative when Arnold is ironic, too dependent on the earnestness of which Arnold is too often

still accused. When on his travels with 'Matthew Arnold' of Grub
Street they see the poacher Diggs being brought before the bench on
which are sitting Bottles, Lumpington, and Hittall, Arminius's commentary does not quite convince the reader, though not in quite the
way 'Matthew Arnold' suggests either:

> 'Such a peasant as that wretched old creature,' he said at last, 'is
> peculiar, my dear friend to your country. Only look at that counte-
> nance! Centuries of feudalism have effaced in it every gleam of
> humane life' . . . 'Centuries of fiddle-sticks!' interrupted I (for I
> assure you, Sir, I can stand up to Arminius well enough on a proper
> occasion). 'My dear Arminius, how can you allow yourself to talk
> such rubbish? Gleam of humane life, indeed! do but look at the
> twinkle in the old rogue's eye. He has plenty of life and wits about
> him, has old Diggs, I can assure you; you just try and come round
> him about a pot of beer!' 'The mere cunning of an animal!' retorted
> Arminius.[14]

This is to lead forward to a discussion about the need to school Diggs's
children, but even without that issue Arminius at least agrees with the
other Matthew Arnold, apparently, that brutality of life had become
necessary for survival in the populace: 'humane' life is not the same as
'plenty of life' nor a 'gleam' identical to a 'twinkle'. What is wrong
and right with Arminius is 'geist'; his intelligence transforms everything that it sees into a generality, and if 'Matthew Arnold's' indul-
gence of Diggs has something of patronage in it, his allowance for
Diggs as individual at least avoids the trap of giving him 'the mere
cunning of an animal'. The comic irony in 'Matthew Arnold' is his
sense of what constitutes 'proper occasion': *his* over-confidence that at
least with Diggs he is on secure ground is as rash as Arminius's
confidence that he sees the mere product of centuries of feudalism.
Both appeal to assumptions different parties in Arnold's readership—
Radical or sentimental Tory—would seize on, and the point of the
writing is not simply to argue but to disconcert us into asking questions. Neither voice sounds trustworthy.

The major problem in the work, of which the above passage is
typical, is a problem of interpretation, of the accuracy with which the
national signs are to be read. As in *Culture and Anarchy*, Arnold is
interested in the accurate reader who will not see in the truss factory
in Trafalgar Square an instance of civilization, whatever it says about
individual freedom, or who will see that freedom of speech is not

enough if it means freedom to circulate twaddle and lies. Yet
Arminius's earnestness is both a useful goad and an ever-present
danger in Arnold himself to offer a kind of over-determination of
meaning (even in old Diggs). As a Thunder ten Tronckh he belongs to
the family that bred Candide. At the end of his first letter (Letter ii) he
reminds the editor of the *Pall Mall* of his ancestry and evinces an
ironical vanity about his aristocratic descent. This misplaced solemnity follows on his earnest response to 'Matthew Arnold's' light-
hearted reinterpretation of the motto of the Reform Club: ' ''Peace to
our nonsense, retrenchment of our profligate expenditure of clap-
trap, and reform of ourselves''. Whether this is true, or merely a
stroke of my poor friend's so-called playfulness (Heaven save the
mark!), I do not feel quite sure; I hope for your sakes it is true, as this is
the very thing you want, and nothing else can save you from certain
decline!'[15] We would all agree with the sentiments but might think that
laughter and playfulness were, even as here, a better defence than
Arminius's trust in an institution or his fatal incapacity to recognize a
joke. German example can stimulate, but in the end salvation comes,
if at all, from within the culture itself, as Burke had argued, through
the native play of irony and deftness of laughter. When Arminius says,
'The worst of it is, I do not see how things are to get better with you at
present', the irony is that he says this in a book which by its style is
trying to develop the mind of the reader so that things will actually be
better. Arminius shares the inability to respond to style with the other
characters in the work, even if less disastrously than Bottles or Hittall.

In the end Arnold asks a lot of his reader, but his insistence that we
respond to a style that negotiates between mockery and feeling, slightness and substance, is the idea beyond all other ideas in the work.
Writing should be able to alter the mind of the reader, not simply by its
ideas, but by the process of thinking it involves. Arminius tries to
induct 'Matthew Arnold' into Hegel, but seems to have found a better
pupil in a fictional Frederick Harrison, reading a fictional 'Phenomenology of *Geist*', appropriately. This is the Harrison whose considered complaint about Arnold was that 'we seek in vain in Mr Arnold
a system of philosophy with principles coherent, interdependent and
derivative'.[16] Maybe, but the nimbleness of mind, the detachment,
the capacity never to surrender to the partial, the priority of questioning over answering, is a task to which literature seems more specifically directed than philosophy. *Friendship's Garland* is a kind of
gymnasium of the controversial style which alters what the reader
thinks controversy is about. The 'ideas', for example, in the earlier

essay 'My Countrymen', appearing in the form, 'This is what British opinions look like from Europe', become trebly complicated when placed *after* the letters and reinterpreted as the *first fruits* of 'Matthew Arnold's' meeting with the fictional Arminius, and then given a scatter of footnotes in 1871 from the elegiac point of view of the finished work. The original Victorian editions, bound in white with a black border and a gold-embossed motif of lilies arranged in a garland over the motto *Manibus plenis date lilia*, turn the book into an emblem. Satire is often close to elegy, just as anger and grief are related emotions. Both forms respond to the presence of death in the world, satire with laughter and elegy with tears. The plight of England and, beyond that, of Europe leaves Arnold moving between the two positions even in this fundamentally comic work. The overstatement with which the work ends, 'Farewell Arminius! Thou good soul, thou great intellect, farewell!'[17] displaces solemnity by laughter. 'Good' and 'great', however, remain serious words, words Arnold would want to retain as current; that 'Matthew Arnold' should attribute them to the man with whom he had such an awkward, tetchy, and discontinuous friendship is partly a comic exposure of funeral customs, yet another instance of a reduced level of public cultivation. But that they should be offered as an epitaph to honest Arminius, who would have denied that he deserved them out of respect for the qualities themselves, is a melancholy recognition that 'goodness' and 'greatness' are maybe the true subjects of the elegy. As in most irony, the work points to what is not there.

Irony in Arnold is an instrument of exactness, and his exactness usually means being clear about what he is *not* saying. He puts himself into positions that can be easily misunderstood. He will write enthusiastically on the function of the French Academy and English readers will immediately think he is recommending it as a model for the English. He will write about *Celtic Literature* not to defend the Welsh language or institutions like the *eisteddfod*, but to urge that there are qualities in Celtic culture which have become part of the British habit of mind, and which those who think of themselves as Anglo-Saxons should recognize within themselves. He will give a lecture in Emerson's birthplace, inspired by admiration, yes, but will then spend two-thirds of the lecture explaining that Emerson is not a philosopher and not even a good prose writer. It is not simply that what he writes was often misunderstood; he writes to court misunderstanding: his relation to the reader is to prepare him for disappointment, for the issues being more complex than he had thought, for the distinctions . being finer than he realized.

It is not simply that Arnold resists the current of his time; he resists those who are resisting the current of time. The desire to find solutions produced in other writers a straighter discourse than Arnold felt he could afford; other men's solutions were for him a part of the problem. The ironical writer must be able to share with the reader a point of view that can distinguish between usages of words being truer or falser. It was maybe the more heterogeneous readership at the time which also made Victorian writers less willing to use irony than Swift and Gay and Fielding and Gibbon. The ironies of Thackeray or the first chapter of Dickens's *Martin Chuzzlewit* seem straightforward affairs when compared with a chapter of *Tom Jones* or *Tristram Shandy*. Maybe also the Victorian writer's desire to use old languages in new ways, especially religious concepts for moral or psychological states, displaces irony; both are saying one thing but implying another. Arnold often turns that process upside down. Authentic religious belief, he will maintain, always *had* been 'morality touched by emotion', and to think it anything else had been an historical misreading. From that point of view nothing had changed, and what had been believed was still believed; all that had changed was our understanding of what religious belief involved. The line of argument must have been puzzling to the contemporary reader.

The fastidiously sceptical point of view in Arnold needs the protection of its irony. What is to be an important voice in the prose works finds its fullest expression in *Friendship's Garland*. As so often in his work, the buried life of the composition does not reveal its oracle in so many words. The role of the style is to command attention, to remind us of the surrounding Babel, to demand a hearing and a social place for intelligence, concentration, and flair by creating them in the act of writing. But irony has also a personal function for Arnold. It is a mode that makes the reader anxious, but anxious for understanding, not for himself. Irony has an impersonality which fends off the introspective or the confessional. The gap we notice in Arnold's poems between surface clarity and inner dilemma is resolved in irony. The problem he identifies so many times in the poems, that the contemporary mind becomes dissipated 'by a continual dance of ever-changing objects'[18] to which he himself also surrenders—'at the central point I am too apt to hoist up the mainsail to the wind and let her drive—'[19] is resolved by irony, which can be heterogeneous while mocking mere heterogeneity and can inhabit the frame of mind which it is also criticizing. The critical distance remains constant, the style valiantly cool, while the mind engages its multifarious opponents without and within.

Irony maintains simultaneously a confident laughter and a sceptical reserve.

Notes

1 *CPW* v 44. R. H. Super has, with some stated misgivings, decided to organize the material of *Friendship's Garland* in terms of its chronology. The argument of this essay depends, however, on the emblematic order of the original volume, which follows a different plan. I shall, therefore, include page references also to the original edition (actually, in this case the second edition). The reference here to this edition, then, is *Friendship's Garland* (1897), 14 (hereafter *FG*).

2 *Discourses in America* (1885), 166; *CPW* x 171, 173–4, 176.

3 *CPW* v 174.

4 Frederic Harrison, *Tennyson, Ruskin, Mill* (1899), 130.

5 [The marked difference between Arnold's distinctive free-running style in his early letters to Clough (*CL*) and his more formal manner in letters to other correspondents, including members of his own family (many of them first gathered and discreetly edited by George Russell in 1895), has always been a matter of note. The difference is confirmed by what has been learned from recent study of the manuscripts, especially by Professor Cecil Lang in preparing his forthcoming and eagerly awaited comprehensive edition of Arnold's letters.—editor's note.]

6 *Five Uncollected Essays*, ed. Kenneth Allott (Liverpool, 1953), 23; *CPW* x 194.

7 *God and the Bible* (1875), 14; *CPW* vii 161.

8 Ibid., 86; *CPW* vii 227.

9 *Letters* i 390, 450, 457.

10 Five Uncollected Essays, 79; *CPW* x 74.

11 *CPW* v 40; *FG* 8.

12 *Letters* i 399.

13 *CPW* v 41; *FG* 10.

14 *CPW* v 67–8; *FG* 47–8.

15 *CPW* v 46–7; *FG* 18.

16 *CPW* v 76; *FG* 63.

17 *CPW* v 36; *FG* 172.

18 See the Yale Manuscript, cited R. H. Super, *The Time Spirit of Matthew Arnold* (Ann Arbor: University of Michigan Press 1970), 16.

19 Letter to Clough, 23 September, 1849 (*CL* 111).

"What You Feel, I Share": Breaking the Dialogue of the Mind with Itself

JOHN P. FARRELL

It would be difficult to find a discussion of Matthew Arnold's critique of modern life and modern sensibility that did not emphatically refer us to his 1853 Preface and to his famous phrase about 'the dialogue of the mind with itself'. This internal colloquy Arnold identified as one of the potentially debilitating characteristics of modern life. In offering his diagnosis, he not only produced what is sometimes too readily used as a hallmark term for the isolation and alienation reflected in modern literature generally, he also, of course, produced a ready-made term for the critical analysis of his own poetry. The poems have been explored in quite illuminating ways as instances of 'the dialogue of the mind with itself'. And yet, as Kenneth Burke would always remind us, every way of seeing is also a way of not seeing. Our preoccupation with the mind's imprisoning dialogue in Arnold's poetry has often diminished critical perception of his attempts to break free of the prison and to encounter the other, to communicate himself to another. The very passage in which his famous phrase appears suggests the ambiguous status of the 'dialogue' in Arnold's mind. 'What those who are familiar only with the great monuments of early Greek genius suppose to be its exclusive characteristics, have disappeared: the calm, the cheerfulness, the disinterested objectivity have disappeared; the dialogue of the mind with itself has commenced; modern problems have presented themselves; we hear already the doubts, we witness the discouragement, of Hamlet and of Faust'.[1]

The passage points in two different directions: inwardly, to a heart of darkness where thought moves in a wearying, dispiriting dialectic; and, outwardly, to an audience of witnesses who understand and recognize—'*hear*'—the dialogue of the mind with itself. The witnesses are all those who share Arnold's view of modernism's trials, who are versed in its typical texts, and who are linked, evidently, by these very assumptions to Arnold himself. The inward and outward directions of the passage are both important. Arnold's poetry explores the dispiriting dialectic of the mind with itself, but it also explores the possibilities of exit, encounter, and engagement. I am not referring here to poems like 'Heine's Grave', in which the scene of isolation and unrelieved self-consciousness is rejected by a speaker who boldly dissociates himself from a life that is 'Bitter and strange' and seeks 'a life/Other and milder' (ll.223, 226). Arnold's conscious yearning for a 'wholeness based on intellectual and moral mastery of a complex "modern" consciousness' is a decisive and widely recognized aspect of his poetry and his poetic career.[2] But there is a dimension of Arnold's poetry that carries out his escape from isolation in a less intellectually prescriptive and less emotionally narrowed form. What Arnold projects, in this other dimension, is rather closer to the double-movement we have seen in his plangent description of the mind's dialogue with itself: he simultaneously speaks in a voice voided by enclosure and a voice quickened by encounter.

Another way of putting the same point is to say that in Arnold's poetry we often find the dialectic of the mind accompanied by dialogue with an absent other, a figure whom Arnold's speaker turns to, addresses, and engages in discourse even when this 'other' remains more or less a figment. The most compelling instance of this strategy in all of Arnold's poetry occurs, in fact, in *Empedocles* itself. At the only moment in the poem when Empedocles evinces any sense of exaltation, he says:

> And yet what days were those,
>   Parmenides!
> When we were young, when we could
>   number friends
> In all the Italian cities like ourselves,
> When with elated hearts we joined your train,
> Ye Sun-born Virgins! on the road of truth.
> Then we could still enjoy, then neither
>   thought
> Nor outward things were closed
>   and dead to us;
> But we received the shock of mighty
>   thoughts
> On simple minds with a pure
>   natural joy.[3]

Empedocles here addresses another poet-philosopher who shared with him the experience of an intellectual dialectic that exhilarated, rather than depressed the mind. The joy that Empedocles remembers depends as much on his sense of companionship in the search for truth as on the 'mighty thoughts' he and his companions received. Two other points should be noted as well. Empedocles speaks directly to his kindred spirit, Parmenides, even though it is the absence of Parmenides that makes the scene so poignant. And, in his address to Parmenides, Empedocles speaks the thoughts of his mentor. This is made clear by the phrases about the 'Sun-born Virgins' and 'the road of truth' which are *topoi* from the hexameter poem in which the historical Parmenides narrated his philosophy of being. Arnold underscored the borrowing in 1867 when he added a note to the lines in question referring his reader to Parmenides' poem. As I will argue presently, these echoings and quotations involve much more than academic punctiliousness. They involve, at bottom, Arnold's nurturing of his intersubjective self, his faith in the structures of language, literature, and culture to facilitate the self's access to the other.

Before I develop this view, I wish to consider a somewhat different approach to the same questions. The most sensitive reading of Arnold's effort to overcome the circular dialogue of the mind is William A. Madden's discussion of the poems, especially those in the 'Switzerland' series, that construct direct dialogues with a beloved. Madden finds that in such poems the crucial experience is 'the discovery that union with another through love, or knowledge, is rare if not impossible.' Moreover, this discovery leads in time to a recognition 'that it is scarcely possible even to know oneself.'⁴ In a particularly trenchant comment, Madden compares Arnold's love poems to the Clough letters and concludes that both the poetic and the epistolary sequences 'reveal a consciousness exploring itself in the presence of another rather than in communion with the other.'⁵

The difference between Arnold's exploring himself in the presence of another rather than in communion with another is quite fundamental. But while Arnold only fitfully succeeds, as 'The Buried Life' testifies, in finding his way to the other person through love, he is not altogether without alternative resources. Though he rarely achieves the intensity of connection that the love poems desire, there yet occurs for Arnold a genuine connection that moves him from isolated self-exploration to a deeply experienced communion. The form of this communion is, in a special sense, intellectually conversational. Arnold internalizes the discursive expression of another, reproduces it, and projects into the world around him the drama of his encounter with a *comprehending* companion.

If Arnold's letters to Clough often move us because they reflect his difficulties in attaining communion with another, his letters to his sister Jane ('K') suggest the closer, more interdependent relationships that Arnold could, at times, construct in his poetry. Writing, probably, in the winter of 1849–50, he addresses Jane as an ideal, responsive partner who has enabled him to imagine and then to enact his escape from paralyzing isolation:

> I am subject to these periods of spiritual eastwind when I can lay hold only of the outside of events or words. . . . You my darling have been a refreshing thought to me in my dryest periods: I may say that you have been one of the most faithful witnesses (almost the only one after papa) among those with whom I have lived & spoken of the reality & possibility of that abiding inward life which we all desire, most of us talk about & few possess.[6]

These are not light words, nor is Arnold's comment in another letter: 'I never think a performance of mine is fairly launched until I have your opinion of it. . . . You generally lay your finger on points where at any rate I can understand what you mean, which one cannot always do apropos of one's critics' objections.'[7]

Arnold is clearly casting his sister in the role of an ideal reader, one whom he can summon up in his imagination (as a 'refreshing thought') to act as authenticating witness to the reality of his buried self. It is only through such authentication that the buried self can surge beyond the mind's dialogue and externalize its presence or experience its true nature. In the role of ideal reader, Arnold's sister could reflect back to him the difference between an empty colloquy of the mind and a resonant conversation with another. If Arnold was unable to move toward resonant conversation in the love poems, he was at least able to do so in situations where he could model authentic communion on the literary interchanges, the conversations of authors and auditors, that form so dominant a part of his poetry. The poems that successfully dramatize conversations of this kind may be said to suspend the dialogue of the mind with itself in favor of a *dialogism* that releases the isolated self and opens the way toward the communion that Empedocles once experienced with Parmenides and that, in another form, Arnold himself experienced with his sister Jane.

Dialogism is a term now almost exclusively associated with the writings of the Russian critic Mikhail Bakhtin (1895–1975). Bakhtin has, in recent years, become extraordinarily influential. He has explored, cogently and imaginatively, the complex ways in which our language practices attempt to deal with the pluralism and flux of our experience. At the heart of his thought is his consideration of the personal and social dynamics that make human dialogue possible. He conceives of 'dialogue', comprehensively, as the intricate set of conditions—social, linguistic, psychological, cultural—that attend any actual exchange between persons. 'Dialogism' is a term which attempts to capture the contingencies and the plurality of voices that are orchestrated, consciously and unconsciously, in our discourse. Indeed, discourse of all kinds appears in Bakhtin as, essentially, conversation.

Many of Arnold's poems are dialogic, even when no ordinary 'dialogue' is shown. For example, 'Self-Dependence' dramatizes a speaker who addresses the stars and enters into 'conversation' with them. The poem begins, however, with the speaker considering, in classic Arnoldian fashion, the enervating effects of the 'dialogue of the mind with itself'.

> Weary of myself, and sick of asking
> What I am, and what I ought to be,
> At this vessel's prow I stand, which bears me,
> Forwards, forwards, o'er the starlit sea.

The image of 'the starlit sea' is a turning point in the poem because it leads the speaker away from his internal dialogue to his conversation with the stars. The dialogue situation in Bakhtin's sense is already at play because, as Bakhtin suggests in many different ways, one of the critical stresses in our practice of language comes from the inherent tensions of mind confronting matter or the subject confronting nature. The exchange between individuals is always, to some degree, informed and framed by our entire experience of consciousness trying to embrace the resisting otherness of the world. The speaker in 'Self-Dependence' immediately moves to overcome his separation from the stars by gazing at them in 'passionate desire' (l. 5). Then something quite telling occurs. Though the estranged man describes himself as *gazing*, he actually is *speaking* (the following words):

> Ye who from my childhood up have calm'd me,
> Calm me, ah, compose me to the end!

> (ll. 7–8)

There is no transition whatever from the poet's gazing to his speaking. His looks are a language. The point of emphasizing the moment of the gaze in the poem is not to call attention to some hidden subtlety of theme or meaning, but rather to underline the complete naturalness of what occurs. The poet makes his looks a language because stars themselves do not speak. They look. The sense of the rest of the poem depends entirely on our understanding that the speaker is translating a language of looks into words. The speaker has found a way to converse with the stars, to form his utterance in dialogic relation to the utterance of the stars, to enact a conversation in spite of the stars' sublime silence. In fact it is the very sublimity of this silence that, paradoxically, renders the stars articulate. Or nearly articulate. Arnold does not propose that the stars speak. Instead, as the speaker's gaze gives him some feeling of an enlarged life, there comes to him 'In the rustling night-air', an unidentified voice which does speak and which tells him that he should *live* as the stars live:

> Unaffrighted by the silence round them,
> Undistracted by the sights they see,
> These demand not that the things without them
> Yield them love, amusement, sympathy.

(ll. 17–20)

Whose utterance is this? We cannot know. The voice is deliberately undefined and unplaced. Except for the 'rustling' in the night-air, it has no auditory vehicle. It is an internal voice situated, untraceably, in the external world, as though the collective wisdom of the ages can be heard, not in language but in the night air, just as the speaker can converse in gazes with the stars.

The questions *who* is speaking, *how* does speaking, occur, and *what* conditions surround and impinge on our acts of communication are basic to Bakhtin's notion of dialogism. In any act of communication there is a constant interplay of individual performances, cultural systems, real and imagined discourses, and modes of expression, both verbal and non-verbal, that inevitably makes our utterances polyphonic. Our simplest statements may be the locus of multiple voices. Self-development is thus always a matter of intersections with other selves and assimilations of other forms of utterance. One can only look at one's self in the reflections of others; one can only hear one's self in the voices of others. Identity is thus always an archetectonic relation between the individual's unique position and the constantly changing social, natural, and cultural environment that is, at once, both speaking in the self and reconstituting the self's speech. Language, Bakhtin argues, 'lies on the border between oneself and the other. The word in language is half someone else's. It becomes "one's own" only when the speaker populates it with his own intention, his own account.'[8] In consequence, the individual consciousness 'finds itself inevitably facing the necessity of *having to choose a language*', and in the very act of choosing, one forms an alliance.[9]

The alliance made in 'Self-Dependence' is paradigmatic for Arnold's poetry. The poem's title refers to its theme: the speaker must learn to overcome his restless self-consciousness and imitate the abiding poise and self-containment of the stars.

> Bounded by themselves, and unregardful
> In what state God's other works may be,
> In their own tasks all their powers pouring,
> These attain the mighty life you see.
>
> (ll. 25–8)

But the poem, at the very peak of its Emersonian resolve, turns into a dialogic performance. The poet only finds himself by gazing at the stars and discovering the form of their utterance to him. Even the lesson he is to learn—how to imitate the stars which are 'Undistracted by the sights they see' (l. 18)—does not reach him until he disrupts his initial mood of internal colloquy and begins to imagine himself in dialogue. Moreover, the voice that comes to him, the voice of prophetic wisdom, is, precisely, his own voice sedimented with cultural texts that speak through him in order to speak to him.

> O air-born voice! long since, severely clear,
> A cry like thine in mine own heart I hear
>
> (ll. 25–9)

Arnold's move toward 'self-dependence' is, then, both an engagement and a disengagement. The poem seeks the condition of anti-self-consciousness only for the purpose of breaking the mind's dialogue with itself. The counter-movement of the poem is to deepen dialogue, to make the aloof stars speak, to listen for voices in the rustling wind, to utter the buried life, to echo words of the other, to respond to the self's dependencies on other selves. Another poem, 'To a Republican Friend, 1848,' concludes with a line that names a recurring assertion in Arnold's poetry: 'What you feel, I share'.

Arnold certainly felt isolated and clearly experienced a drama of rejection as he tried to fit himself into his historical time or find himself reflected in his natural and cultural environment. But his recourse was not, as he himself said, to long for Empedoclean oblivion. Instead, the severity of Arnold's estrangement generated, dialectically, a searching study of how contact and connection might occur. The line I have quoted just now and also used in the title of this paper suggests the degree to which Arnold shares with Bakhtin the contention that 'everything internal gravitates not toward itself but is turned to the outside and dialogized, every internal experience ends up on the boundary'. In other words, even a dialogue of the mind with itself will push the self beyond solitude and prompt the *solitaire* to a dialogic interaction. 'The very being of man (both external and internal) is the *deepest communion. To be* means *to communicate.*'[10]

An extremely interesting and illuminating example of how Arnold's poetry can be approached from Bakhtin's perspective is provided by the figure of Etienne Pivert de Senancour as an absent other in Arnold's work, the poetry as well as the prose, and whose text, *Obermann*, became the centre-point of a complex dialogue that allowed Arnold to free himself from his sense of isolation and re-imagine himself as speaking to '*someone actually present*, someone who hears him and is *capable of answering him.*'[11] In this respect, it is important to remember, as Kenneth Allott has demonstrated, that the figures of Empedocles and Senancour are counterparts in Arnold's poetic world. Both are gripped by modern *ennui*.[12] Arnold situated both of them in forbidding locales. However, while the ashen summit of Etna images the barren internal colloquy that condemns Empedocles to his tragic isolation, Senancour's mountain is a place where voices do interlace and where discourse becomes redeeming.

'Stanzas in Memory of the Author of "Obermann" ' was written in the autumn of 1849, and it begins with Arnold's evocation of the Alpine fastness where Senancour locates Obermann, his fictional persona. Arnold's description of the vast scene breaks off abruptly:

—Yes, Obermann, all speaks of thee;
I feel thee near once more.

(ll. 11–12)

These lines, simple enough in themselves, allude to an involved context surrounding the poem, since the speaker is identifying himself as one already perfectly familiar with Obermann. The surrounding context will help us to recognize the deeply dialogic or polyphonic quality of the poem. Of course, that quality is sharply evident in the poem itself, for its radical opposition is the contrast between the terrible remoteness of the scene and the striking intimacy of communication that unites the figures who inhabit it. Nevertheless, the surrounding context gives us an even clearer account of what is at stake in the poem. Arnold formally recognized this feature of his poem when, in late editions, he himself supplied a sketch of the context by adding a prose headnote to the poetic text. The headnote highlights the bond of familiarity that the original poem had taken for granted.

The headnote brims with significant material, but we will have to confine ourselves to three key points. The first point is its deliberate shunning of Lord Byron. Here the headnote follows the lead of 'Stanzas', one of whose main, but unacknowledged purposes is to curtail the power of Byron's voice. The extraordinary influence of Byron on Arnold, and the anxiety the influence caused him, is well documented.[13] In *Empedocles on Etna* Arnold relied heavily on allusions to Byron in order to define Empedocles's bitterness and despair. But, though still compelled by Byron, Arnold was trying to heroicize a milder, more sympathetic version of *ennui* in Senancour. Part of Senancour's appeal for Arnold was his appropriation of a symbolic site that Byron had identified imperiously with his own version of gloom. Arnold's need to replace Byron with Senancour as the presiding Alpine spirit was intensified by the fact that the journey of September 24–27, 1849, that inspired Arnold's first poem on Senancour, retraced a segment of Byron's travels in the Alps. The details of Byron's itinerary were given in the guidebook Arnold carried with him, John Murray's *Handbook to Switzerland*. Arnold's emotional effort to cast off Byron is clearly reflected in the hyperbole of an attack on Byron that he made in a letter he wrote at the time to Clough. The 'whole locality,' Arnold says, 'is spoiled by the omnipresence there of that furiously flaring bethiefed rushlight, the vulgar Byron.'[14] The casting off of Byron continues, incidentally, in the brief essay on *Obermann* that Arnold contributed to *The Academy* in 1868. There he explicitly identifies Byron as a poser in comparison to Senancour's authenticity (*CPW* v 296).

There is much more to be said on this matter, but the main point is that Arnold's creation of Senancour as a poetic hero is dialogically framed by an unspoken exorcism of Byron. Arnold closes his Byron, as Carlyle advised, but instead of opening his Goethe, an option that 'Stanzas' specifically rejects (ll. 55–68), he initiates a dialogue with Senancour, who had Byron's passionate character, melancholy temperament, and existential isolation, but in a de-eroticized and attractively Pascalian nature. The first bond that facilitates the dialogic relations of Obermann and Arnold's speaker is simply, but very significantly, their shared ability (or desire) to occupy inevitable Byronic spaces without yielding to Byron's malaise.

The second critically contextual point that Arnold offers in his headnote to the *Obermann* poems is his explicit dissociation of Senancour from the 'sentimental school' of his European contemporaries, Chateaubriand and Madame de Staël in particular. 'Senancour has a gravity and severity which distinguishes him from all other writers of the sentimental school. The world is with him in his solitude far less than it is with them; of all writers he is the most perfectly isolated and the least attitudinising.' These remarks are also casting a cold eye on Byron, but Arnold is here chiefly concerned with establishing Senancour's sincerity. Senancour's detachment from the world has an ascetic quality which makes him 'perfectly' isolated. Arnold stresses these qualities because the terms he uses set up an emotional and polemical link to the headnote's major claim for Senancour, one that is very nearly paradoxical:

> His chief work . . . has a value and power of its own, apart from these merits of its author. The stir of all the main forces, by which modern life is and has been impelled, lives in the letters of *Obermann*; the dissolving agencies of the eighteenth century, the fiery storm of the French Revolution, the first faint promise and dawn of that new world which our own time is but now more fully bringing to light— all these are to be felt, almost to be touched, there.

The potential paradox involves, of course, Arnold's conversion of his isolated Alpine hero into a master of historical consciousness. But Arnold serves no paradox because in his view the ascetic, severe, 'perfect' quality of Obermann's isolation means that he encodes the several voices of the *Zietgeist* faithfully, leaving his text untinctured by any wayward egotism or mere modishness. Arnold's claim is extremely audacious, and is the equivalent to the claim in 'Stanzas' that Senancour, not Wordsworth or Goethe, is, provisionally, the safest guide for those who have been swept up in the powerful negatives and faint hopes of the modern age. Behind these claims is Arnold's conviction that his own poetic discourse has the same pure and uncompromising recognition of the modern spirit that he finds in Senancour. Senancour and Arnold thus become allies in a project whose *content* is authentic representation of modernism's doubts and discouragements, but whose *form*, which Bakhtin would regard as 'co-consciousness', transcends the frequently embittering dialogue of the mind with itself.[15]

The third point of context, which actually comes first in the head-note, implicitly comments on the central theme of 'Stanzas'. In the poem the speaker comes to a point in his address to Obermann when he announces that he must live in the world and thus, in a sense, repudiate Obermann's reclusiveness. However, a deeper bond with Obermann is immediately forged: Obermann, together with a 'small, transfigured band', ultimately to include Arnold himself, form a new alliance, 'The Children of the Second Birth' (l. 143). The headnote enforces the primacy of this theme by representing just such a 'band' as the few but knowing and appreciative readers of Senancour. The 'profound inwardness' and 'austere sincerity' of *Obermann* 'have attracted and charmed some of the most remarkable spirits of this century, such as George Sand and Sainte-Beuve, and will probably always find a certain number of spirits whom they touch and interest'. In *The Academy* article these 'spirits' are redefined as 'friends [who] will never fail him' (*CPW* v 303).

Arnold's emphasis is unmistakable. Senancour's fictional figure, Obermann, is the coalescing agent of a partly imagined and partly real set of secret sharers who produce a dialogically integrated world of responding and corresponding selves. This process was already exemplified before Arnold knew about Senancour. In 1833 Sainte-Beuve was writing an essay about Senancour, and he interested George Sand in *Obermann*. In the same year George Sand composed *Lélia*, a novel that 'could also quite fairly be called *La Pensée de Senancour*'.[16] The novel possessed Arnold's youthful imagination. 'How the sentences from George Sand's works of that period still linger in our memory and haunt the ear with their cadences' (*CPW* viii 220). From George Sand's novel Arnold learned of Senancour. From this followed his meeting with George Sand and his friendship and correspondence with Sainte-Beuve. All of this is only to say that Arnold both wrote and used 'Stanzas in Memory of the Author of "Obermann" ' in response to a sense of shared participation in a world where a group of kindred 'spirits' were internalizing each other's language, creating inter-dependent texts, echoing 'cadences', and forming a discourse not out of the mind's lonely isolation but out of the word's communicative power. Arnold's poems on Senancour emerge from, and look toward, the formation of a common understanding. They are, quite specifi-cally, what Bakhtin means by 'utterances': 'Each utterance is filled

with echoes and reverberations of other utterances to which it is
related. . . . Every utterance must be regarded primarily as a *response*
to preceding utterances of the given sphere.'[17] Even Arnold's attempt
to silence his Byronic voice must be viewed as part of the dynamic
interplay of utterances that converge in the *Obermann* poems.[18]

Arnold's poetic strategies in the *Obermann* poems are dominated by
his search for dialogical alliance. He attempts to make his poems
responsive utterances that play off Senancour's text. Senancour composed *Obermann* in epistolary form; the 'letters' are addressed to a
distant correspondent. Arnold clearly takes on the role of the figure
addressed and thus situates himself as Obermann's ideal reader. But
he also, of course, takes on the role of Obermann himself. What we see
in Arnold's poems is an exchange of discourses through which Arnold
projects himself as Obermann's disciple while the figure of Obermann,
in the structure of each poem, grows more and more Arnoldian. We
have already seen this exchange of discourses in the rhetoric of the
headnote as Arnold both identifies himself with Obermann's detachment and yet assimilates Obermann to a highly Arnoldian reading of
history.

The initial stage of exchange in 'Stanzas' occurs when Arnold's
persona positions himself as a reader who has carried *Obermann* with
him on his Alpine ascent:

> I turn thy leaves! I feel their breath
> Once more upon me roll;
> . . . .
> A fever in these pages burns
> Beneath the calm they feign.

(ll. 13–14; 21–2)

The process of the poem gradually re-shapes Arnold's persona from a
solitary, memorializing reader into one who can engage Obermann in
speech. As a reader, the Arnoldian figure remembers Wordsworth
and Goethe and considers them as potential guides, but finds both less
adequate than Senancour. As writers, Wordsworth and Goethe were,
of course, supremely more important to Arnold than Senancour. Yet
the poem is completely willing to minimize the importance of these
sages for the sake of elevating what Arnold immediately portrays as
the intimacy of access he has to Senancour. Wordsworth and Goethe
are accessible only in their written works, but Senancour seems available to Arnold as a speaking partner, one who addresses Arnold (and

whom Arnold addresses) with care and concern about his differences
and needs. It is just at the point where Arnold's persona realizes his
distance from Wordsworth and Goethe that he begins to 'hear' (1. 90)
Obermann.

More importantly, Arnold represents his own discourse as an
address that Obermann hears. And just as Obermann seems to speak
directly to one phase of Arnold's deepest self, Arnold can reply to
Obermann from yet another phase.

> Away the dreams that but deceive
> And thou, sad guide, adieu!
> I go, fate drives me; but I leave
> Half of my life with you
>
> (ll. 129–32)

Arnold's announcement, of course, is that he nows sees himself as
rejecting Senancour's reclusiveness and committing himself to the
world of action. But this decision does not alter Arnold's devotion to
Senancour. Instead, Arnold's speaker begins to see Senancour as an
increasingly Arnoldian ally whose spirit is to be located not in mountain solitude but among a community of kindred selves,

> Whose one bond is, that all have been
> Unspotted by the world.
>
> (ll. 155–6)

The poem's central action is, then, an exchange of positions: it
begins with Arnold moving toward Senancour; it ends with Senancour
moving toward Arnold. The medium of this movement is the appropriation by each of the other's discourse. Only when the central action
is complete do we discover that the poem is, formally, an elegy. In
other words, it is only when Arnold has shown that Obermann is alive
and accessible in 'that small, transfigured band' whose united utterance is voiced in Arnold's poetry that the poem recognizes Senancour's death and disappearance. The elegy itself is also dual; Arnold is
bidding farewell not only to the deceased Senancour but also to the
solitaire in himself. Yet the poem's action comprehends the final relation of Arnold and Senancour not as a rupture but as a deepened
co-consciousness. The speaker in Arnold's poem has difficulty in
determining where Senancour is buried, and this is a sign that

Senancour's textual voice is now mingled with Arnold's in dialogic partnership.

Some twenty years later Arnold produced his second poem on Senancour, 'Obermann Once More' which, as all critics agree, is more concerned with confirming than with exploring the course of action Arnold had taken since the emotional crises of his early poetry. One hint of the equilibrium Arnold had reached is that 'Obermann Once More' refers unself-consciously to Byron (l. 24). But an altogether more imposing and revealing sign of the new situation is that Arnold openly and extensively converts Obermann's speech into his own. Arnold sees himself as etched with Obermann's language: 'Still in my soul the voice I heard/Of Obermann' (ll. 333-4). However, what we as readers of the poem principally see is the acting out of the process by which Arnold and Obermann engage with each other through a common historical discourse.

The scene of the poem repeats that of 'Stanzas', and once again Arnold's persona senses the presence of Obermann. But this time the persona carries no written text. The natural setting itself is sufficient to suggest Obermann's proximity:

> And who but thou must be, in truth,
>   Obermann! with me here?

(ll. 37-8)

The speaker reviews his separation from Obermann and now treats the separation as though it had been quite unmitigated. But suddenly, wraith-like, Obermann appears.

> A mountain-flower was in his hand,
> A book was in his breast.
> Bent on my face, with gaze which scanned
> My soul, his eyes did rest

(ll. 65-8)

Obermann's reading of Arnold's face, in which he sees lines of hope, becomes the prelude to an historical discourse of nearly three-hundred lines that concludes with a generous assessment of the present time:

> Despair not thou as I despaired,
> Nor be cold gloom thy prison!
> Forward the gracious hours have fared,
> And see! the sun is risen!

(ll. 281-5)

The details of the historical discourse need not be reviewed here; the decisive point is that the whole discourse is founded on Arnold's historical vision. Senancour becomes a co-creator of the humanistic historicism that Arnold had fashioned as a critic and that became the grounds of his tentative *rapprochement* with the modern spirit. Obermann's Arnoldian utterance becomes, through its co-created quality, a figure for the dialogic bonding of self and other. Senancour and Arnold inscribe each other with the signs of their common pursuit, or, as the poem puts it (in italics):

> '*One common wave of thought and joy*
> *Lifting mankind again.*'

(ll. 323–4)

Such a declaration is far removed from 'the dialogue of the mind with itself', and Arnold does not come to it easily. But he arrives at it through resources inherent in his poetry from the beginning.

It must be emphasized that Arnold's efforts to project the dialogic mediation of self and other never pretend to minimize the formidable barriers to a common pursuit. In 'Obermann Once More', though Obermann speaks Arnold's language, he does so in a vision. When he awakes, 'no/Voice moved' (ll. 327–8). Conversely, Arnold has to journey from the historical universe that circumscribes his identity to the natural universe that circumscribes Obermann's. The universes never merge. As always in Arnold, history and nature remain problematically separated theatres of human experience. And yet in spite of these irreducible obstructions, the two figures assimilate each other's words and speak in voices that resonate with each other's utterance.

We come closest to Arnold's sense of this process in the lines quoted above that describe Obermann as he appears in Arnold's dream: 'A book was in his breast'. The book, as the poem will show, is as much Arnold's writing as it is Senancour's. But as the editors of the *Commentary* suggest, the actual book itself probably belongs to neither but is meant to represent a text, mysteriously given to Obermann, written into an old edition of Plutarch. This text is a moral and philosophical fragment attributed to Aristippus and called in Senancour's work the 'Manuel de Pseusophanes'. The 'Manuel' inspires Obermann with its author's faith in human intelligence, strength, and courage. Obermann reprints it—for the sake of his distant correspondent. In Arnold's copy of Senancour's *Obermann*, the 'Manuel' portion of the text is heavily marked, and its general vision of human possibility is reproduced in the dream-vision of 'Obermann Once More'.[19] The book Obermann carries in his breast is a symbolic text, essentially of unknown origin, where a discourse shaped and shared by many voices, exchanged, enlarged, and echoed by 'a certain number of spirits' who are both authors and readers, remains available as a continuing source of 'One common wave of thought and joy'.

Notes

[1] *CPW* i 1.

[2] William A. Madden, *Matthew Arnold: A Study of the Aesthetic Temperament in Victorian England* (Bloomington, Indiana: Indiana University Press, 1967), 76.

[3] See *Empedocles on Etna*, II 235–43 (*Poems* 196–97).

[4] Madden, 80.

[5] Ibid., 85.

[6] Unpublished letter, first printed in A. Dwight Culler, *Imaginative Reason: The Poetry of Matthew Arnold* (New Haven and London: Yale University Press, 1966), 134. On Arnold's sister 'K', see below p. 106 4n.

[7] *Unpublished Letters of Matthew Arnold*, ed. A. Whitridge (New Haven: Yale University Press, 1923), 41.

[8] M. M. Bakhtin, *The Dialogic Imagination: Four Essays*, ed. Michael Holquist, trans. Caryl Emerson and Michael Holquist (Austin: University of Texas Press, 1981), 293.

[9] Ibid., 295.

[10] Mikhail Bakhtin, *Problems of Dostoevsky's Poetics*, ed. and trans. Caryl Emerson (Minneapolis: University of Minnesota Press, 1984), 286.

[11] Ibid., 63. Italics in the original.

[12] 'A Background for *Empedocles on Etna*,' *Essays and Studies* (n.s. 21, 1968), 86.

[13] See Kenneth Allott, 'Arnold's *Empedocles on Etna* and Byron's "Manfred",' *N&Q* (n.s. 9, 1962), 300–3; Leon Gottfried, *Matthew Arnold and the Romantics* (Lincoln: University of Nebraska Press, 1986), chapter 3; and my 'Arnold, Byron, and Taine', *English Studies* (55, 1974), 435–9. See also in this volume Bernard Beatty, 'Empedocles and Byron Once More' (pp. 80–95).

[14] *CL* 92; and see Culler, 128–129.

[15] For the term "co-consciousness", see Katrina Clark and Michael Holquist, *Mikhail Bakhtin* (Cambridge: Harvard University Press, 1984), 77.

[16] Patricia Thomson, *George Sand and the Victorians* (London: Macmillan, 1977), 98. For the 'ineffaceable impression *Lélia* made on Arnold,' see Thomson's discussion, 97–109, and in this volume Ruth apRoberts, 'Arnold and George Sand' (pp. 96–107).

[17] M. M. Bakhtin, *Speech Genres and Other Late Essays*, trans. V. W. McGee, ed. Caryl Emerson and Michael Holquist (Austin: University of Texas Press), 91.

[18] The matter of intersecting or multiple voices in Arnold's poetry has been examined from different perspectives by W. Stacy Johnson, *The Voices of Matthew Arnold: An Essay on Criticism* (New Haven: Yale University Press, 1961); by Miriam Allott, 'Matthew Arnold; ''All One and Continuous'' ' in *The Victorian Experience: The Poets*, ed. Richard A. Levine (Athens: Ohio University Press, 1981), 67–93; and by Kenneth and Miriam Allott, 'Arnold the Poet: (ii) Narrative and Dramatic Poems' in Kenneth Allott, ed., *Matthew Arnold*, 'Writers and their Background' (London: Bell & Sons, 1975), 70–71.

[19] For these details, see *Commentary* 266–7.

Arnold's Gift: The Poet in an Unpoetic Age

PHILIP DAVIS

An *incomplete* poet in an *unpoetic* age: that is how to lose twice over, inside and out. 'As deep as his sense that the time was out of joint, was the feeling of this Hamlet that he had no power to set it right . . . so that, unfavourable as may have been his time, we should err in attributing to any outward circumstances the whole of the discouragement by which he is pervaded.' This is Arnold on Senancour, the poet to whose Obermann he pays tribute in two celebrated poems.[1] But it is also Arnold himself, for Arnold was a poet whose perception of his own poetic incompleteness itself seems to have furthered, almost as a consequence, the diminution of his ability to write poems. 'For he always had said that poetry was one of the frantic professions in which success depends on the opinion you hold of yourself. Think well of yourself, and you win. Lose self-esteem, and you're finished.' This is the narrator in *Humboldt's Gift* (1975) by Saul Bellow[2], the novelist whose reflections about his modern author's 'gift' have helped to set moving ideas explored in this essay about Arnold's position in relation to Wordsworth—one of the great 'presiders' among his predecessors— and to Hardy, one of his major successors confronting, in his turn, the problematics of poetry 'at the present time'. 'Lose self-esteem, and you're finished': but on what does the opinion you hold of yourself depend? Not just on yourself. There is a vicious circle in all this whereby if a poet's failure is at least partly symptomatic of the state of his age, nonetheless part of that failure lies in his inability adequately to criticize his own times. So, most often, we lose sight of him in that swallowing circle, even though it is in such lesser types that we may see best those problems which the greater resolve or evade. For of the greater type, lesser people will think this:

> In the day's life, whose iron round
> Hems us all in, he is not bound;
> He leaves his kind, o'erleaps their pen,
> And flees the common life of men.
> He escapes thence, but we abide—[3]

Others abide our question. Thou art free![4]

Literary history seems to have decided that of the writers of the two following passages, the first is a lesser, the second a major poet. Yet there is a relation—finer than that of mere contrast—between this:

> . . . we strain on,
> On—and at nightfall at last
> Come to the end of our way,
> To the lonely inn 'mid the rocks;
> Where the gaunt and taciturn host
> Stands on the threshold, the wind,
> Shaking his thin white hairs—
> Holds his lantern to scan
> Our storm-beat figures, and asks:
> Whom in our party we bring?
> Whom we have left in the snow?
>
> Sadly we answer: We bring
> Only ourselves! we lost
> Sight of the rest in the storm.

—from Arnold's 'Rugby Chapel'—and this:

> Who is the third who walks always beside you?
> When I count, there are only you and I together
> But when I look ahead up the white road
> There is always one walking beside you
> Gliding wrapt in a brown mantle, hooded
> I do not know whether a man or a woman.
> —But who is that on the other side of you? . . .

—from T. S. Eliot's *The Waste Land*. Someone, something, not there that should be; someone, something, there and yet missing when counted: it is only that Arnold is more desperate than Eliot to 'count', full on, that makes him look more strainingly prosaic. Yet in Arnold (dare I say) we have a more self-damagingly honest sense of the problem of writing such poetry. 'There are a certain number of personages who have been real men of genius . . . but who, for some reason or other, in most cases for very valid reasons, have remained obscure.' A genius of that kind, says Arnold, often has more for us than greater men.[5]

The story of the incomplete poet still deserves to be told—and is still being told. In *Humboldt's Gift*, the writer Charlie Citrine recalls his

ex-friend, the failed poet Von Humboldt Fleisher, and behind this is
Saul Bellow's own memory of Delmore Schwartz. Here is one of
Citrine's laments for Humboldt:

> The ideas of the last few centuries are used up. . . . The greatest
> things, the things most necessary for life, have recoiled and
> retreated. People are actually dying of this, losing all personal life,
> and the inner being of millions, many many millions, is missing.
> One can understand that in many parts of the world there is no
> hope for it because of famine or police dictatorships, but here in the
> free world what excuse have we? . . . Mankind must recover its
> imaginative powers, recover living thought and real being, no
> longer accept these insults to the soul, and do it soon! Or else! And
> this is where a man like Humboldt, faithful to failed ideas, lost his
> poetry and missed the boat. (pp. 244–5)

'The greatest things . . . have recoiled and retreated': this recalls
Arnold's Sea of Faith on Dover Beach:

> But now I only hear
> Its melancholy, long, withdrawing roar,
> Retreating . . .
>
> (ll. 24–6)

'The inner being of millions, many many millions, is missing':

> Most men eddy about
> Here and there—eat and drink,
> Chatter and love and hate,
> Gather and squander, are raised
> Aloft, are hurled in the dust,
> Striving blindly, achieving
> Nothing . . .
>
> 'Rugby Chapel' (ll. 60–6)

'People are actually dying of this':

> For most men in a brazen prison live,
> Where, in the sun's hot eye,
> Their heads bent o'er their toil, they languidly
> Their lives to some unmeaning taskwork give.
>
> 'A Summer Night' (ll. 37–40)

If they weren't so passive, they would have to see how, even thus 'languidly', they are still actively *giving* their *lives* to unmeaning things. A hundred years on, Arnold seems only as out-of-date as the things that Saul Bellow is still lamenting the loss of.

Yet Arnold was no Humboldt. For what Citrine witnessed in Humboldt was a form of romantic self-destruction, a man trying to symbolize in his own ruin the death of (his) Poetry. But so far from making a victory of defeat, such a gesture (says Citrine) simply played into the hands of America's philistines as exactly what they expected of poets: 'the USA is too tough, too big, too much, too rugged . . . And to be a poet is a school thing, a skirt thing, a church thing. . . . [Poets] can't make it here.' (pp. 117–18) The great danger for America, Arnold had prophesied, lay in its youthful capacity for 'self-glorification and self-deception', and that is precisely how Humboldt had failed in his mission even through exaggerating it.[6] Arnold, resisting the idea of suicide that he put in his poem *Empedocles on Etna*, did not destroy himself—at least not literally:

> And you, ye stars,
> Who slowly begin to marshal,
> As of old, in the fields of heaven,
> Your distant, melancholy lines!
> Have you, too, survived yourselves?
>
> *Empedocles on Etna* (II i 276–80)

The poet became the school inspector; the artist became the critic; the aesthete became a moralist. That was how Arnold, in both senses, equivocally 'survived himself': living on after the death of his best or poetic self; yet surviving the Empedocles or Humboldt in himself. Arnold's career as incomplete poet has always seemed emblematic of a deeply wounding incompatibility between Poetry and the Modern World. But it cannot be said, with romantic simplicity, either that Arnold morally gave up Poetry for the sake of the World and its practical cares, or that the World with its pressures damagingly unfitted him for Poetry. There is something in Arnold more soberly and adultly compromised than the merely dramatic alternatives suggest.

> Ah! two desires toss about
> The poet's feverish blood.

One drives him to the world without,
And one to solitude.
                'In Memory of the Author of "Obermann" ' (ll. 93–6)

The clarity of the opposites is really only a way of speaking of the
more essential confusion in between them—a way of speaking of the
felt *impossibility* yet equally felt *experience* of their division from each
other. The formal poles (Poetry versus the World; Solitude versus
Society) are in fact only *symptoms* of their own content—symptoms of
the very dilemma in between them to which, thus artificially turned
inside-out, they give the space for expression. Arnold always felt like
an in-between man—in history itself 'Wandering between two
worlds, one dead/The other powerless to be born' ('Stanzas from the
Grande Chartreuse'). Being between two worlds like that is intrin-
sically ambiguous: the consciousness of the two worlds hardly leaves
room to exist, unharassed, between them; but the perception of the
space in between them allows no way out of itself—a present that can
become neither the past nor the future both seems non-existent in its
own right and yet painfully exists. It is characteristic of Arnold's
poetry to hold things together *and* to hold them apart in a double
picture of this sort. For it is what Hegel diagnosed as the state of
Unhappy Consciousness—a division within a unity, one half of a split
looking across at its other half as both a part of itself and yet also
alienated from itself.

A borrowed and artificial way of speaking of an otherwise unspeakable dilemma—that is Arnold's use of Poetry. For, again artificially,
Arnold gives Nature a voice in his poem, 'The Youth of Nature.' It is
a voice that says that those individuals, such as Wordsworth, who
have celebrated her, in fact brought to her the very qualities they
celebrated:

'Race after race, man after man,
Have thought that my secret was theirs,
Have dreamed that I lived but for them,
That they were my glory and joy.
—They are dust, they are changed, they are gone!
I remain.' (ll. 129–34)

'I remain,' says Nature, putting man down. But in that magnificently
austere cry, even Nature has to borrow a human voice in order to deny
human relations. Empedocles goes even further:

Man errs not that he deems
His welfare his true aim,
He errs because he dreams
The world does but exist that welfare to bestow. (II i 173–6)

Nature, like History, is one of the great forces whose indifference to its
own human products is a feeling to us—a feeling of denial—but no
more than a fact to it, a fact which denies even the feeling. Nature
gives no direct sanction for human needs. Yet the very perception of
that lack at least lends us, on the rebound, a borrowed sanction for a
stoic independence. Such inferences replace direct causes in the mind
of Empedocles: 'Because thou must not dream,' he tells Pausanias,
'thou need'st not then despair' (I ii 426). 'Because' here means only
'just because', without providing a straight reason. Another of Saul
Bellow's protagonists, Moses Herzog, finds himself madly writing to
Spinoza about just such human ungroundedness and mental loneli-
ness: 'Thoughts not causally connected were said by you to cause
pain. I find that is indeed the case.'[7] In the pain of his almost
unspeakably impossible world, the poetry of a borrowed voice becomes
Arnold's only way of speaking, as it were, inside-out. 'We mortal
millions live *alone*,' he writes in 'To Marguerite—Continued', using
'we' at the very moment of the dissolution of this language into
unshareable, though paradoxically similar, alonenesses (I, you, he,
she). 'The best are silent now,' he cries in 'Stanzas from the Grande
Chartreuse': Poetry is the only voice that can be used to suffer in
silence.

Arnold had no beliefs to put into poetry so much as a belief in Poetry
itself:

Two kinds of *dilettanti*, says Goethe, there are in poetry: he who
neglects the indispensable mechanical part, and thinks he has done
enough if he shows spirituality and feelings; and he who seeks to
arrive at poetry merely by mechanism, in which he can acquire an
artisan's readiness, and is without soul and matter. And he adds,
that the first does most harm to art, and the last to himself. If we
must be *dilettanti*: if it is impossible for us, under the circumstances
amidst which we live, to think clearly, to feel nobly, and to delineate
firmly: if we cannot attain to the mastery of the great artists;—let
us, at least, have so much respect for our art as to prefer it to ourselves. Let us not bewilder our successors; let us transmit to them
the practice of poetry, with its boundaries and wholesome regulative

laws, under which excellent works may again, perhaps, at some future time, be produced.[8]

This was 'at least' the best choice for (to use one of Arnold's own titles) 'The Second Best': to prefer our art to ourselves. Yet if that was Arnold's preference between the two poles of Art and Self, Arnold's gift was to make the choice of the one pole include within itself the loss of the other. By another of his circles, the gift was to make art-preferred-to-self into art about the very loss of self within it, 'without soul and matter'. Again, Arnold was having it both ways,

> One drives him to the world without,
> And one to solitude.
> > 'In Memory of the Author of "Obermann" ' (ll. 95–6)

and was also having it neither way,

> *Never by passion quite possessed*
> *And never quite benumbed by the world's sway . . .*
> > 'A Summer Night' (ll. 32–3)

For Arnold, the very act of putting the dilemma into Poetry makes an invisible difference. What is this difference? 'I cannot tell, and I am not much concerned to know; the important thing is that it does arise, and that we can profit by it'; 'one may say of it as is said of faith: "One must feel it in order to know what it is." '[9] But what it is, this x factor which makes all the difference, the reader of Arnold's own 'Sohrab and Rustum' will know imperfectly. For it is not that this narrative poem defeats our prosaic expectations: the father does unwittingly kill his own son, Sohrab, as we guessed from the very first. There is a subtler difference involved in the way it *does* fulfil our expectations and still somehow manages to take us (in Wordsworth's great phrase) by 'a gentle shock of mild surprise'. It is a difference registered in tiny details, as when Rustum's cry of recognition at the end is, 'O boy—thy father!', not, 'O boy—my son'. The minimal but vital difference of poetry 'at least'.

'When there comes in poetry what I may call the *lyrical cry*, this transfigures everything, makes everything grand.'[10] The ability to write poetry is always for Arnold the crucial sign of the capacity to transform and transcend personal helplessness—in an effort to attain 'the *mastery* of the great artists'. What in Arnold's eyes distinguishes

Chaucer from contemporary French romance-poets is Chaucer's command of a view of the whole of life: 'Chaucer has not their help-lessness; he has gained the power to survey the world from a central, a truly human point of view.'[11] Without that power, 'each half-lives a hundred different lives', in the sick hurry, in the divided aims from which Arnold urges his Scholar-Gipsy to take refuge. What is thus liter-ally vital to Arnold is the creative capacity *not* to suffer; while to be unable to write poetry becomes a most damagingly silent admission of helplessness.

It is in his ability to make writing something other than the recon-struction of suffering that Arnold finds Wordsworth important. 'Wordsworth's poetry is great because of the extraordinary power with which Wordsworth feels the joy offered us in nature, the joy offered to us in the simple primary affections and duties; and because of the extraordinary power with which, in case after case, he shows us this joy, and renders it so as to make us share it.'[12] A favourite case of Arnold's was Michael; I take an example at random:

> Those fields, those hills—what could they less? had laid
> Strong hold on his affections, were to him
> A pleasurable feeling of blind love,
> The pleasure which there is in life itself.
>
> 'Michael' (ll. 74–7)

Arnold coined his critical terms for practical application. If, accord-ingly, we put into practice the distinctions he employs in his essays on Keats and on Maurice de Guérin, it seems to me that the movement from the third line of the above quotation to the fourth is a movement from 'sensuous' to 'spiritual', from 'natural' to 'moral' interpretation. The movement from the adjectival

> A pleasurable feeling of blind love

to the more essential

> The pleasure which there is in life itself

marks something which has both sunk down into Michael's very char-acter, over the years, and been raised up by the ability of the poet 'to take unto the height/The measure of himself'.[13] That is mastery rather than helplessness; that is the interpretative power of poetry: 'by which

I mean, not a power of drawing out in black and white an explanation of the mystery of the universe, but the power of so dealing with things as to awaken in us a wonderfully full, new, and intimate sense of them, and of our relations with them. When this sense is awakened in us, as to objects without us, we feel ourselves to be in contact with the essential nature of those objects, to be no longer bewildered and oppressed by them, but to have their secret, and to be in harmony with them; and this feeling calms and satisfies us as no other can.'[14] No longer 'prevailed over by the world's multitudinousness', we feel through such poetry the pleasure which there is 'in life itself'.[15]

At such moments Wordsworth—to use a crucial word for Arnold—is *adequate*. For 'adequate' is the word Arnold uses again and again in his essay, 'On the Modern Element in Literature', as he searches the literature of the past for a model of intellectual deliverance from the depressed, irritated confusions of the 'democratic' present. At its best, Wordsworth's adequacy both elevates and democratizes; it is 'accesible universally'.[16] And it is the Wordsworth of Margaret (Book 1 of *The Excursion*) that Arnold critically selected as Wordsworth at his best; again I choose my own example and apply to it Arnold's own terms:

> . . . And so she lived
> Through the long winter, reckless and alone;
> Until her house by frost, and thaw, and rain,
> Was sapped; and while she slept, the nightly damps
> Did chill her breast; and in the stormy day
> Her tattered clothes were ruffled by the wind,
> Even at the side of her own fire. Yet still
> She loved this wretched spot, nor would for worlds
> Have parted hence; and still that length of road,
> And this rude bench, one torturing hope endeared,
> Fast rooted at her heart: and here, my Friend,—
> In sickness she remained; and here she died;
> Last human tenant of these ruined walls!
>
> *The Excursion* (ll. 904–16)

While she hopes against hope for her husband's return, the place (like her hope) is killing her; 'yet still' she loves that wretched spot as she loves her husband. What is killing her she is also devoting her life to. 'The connection which suffering has with effort, with exertion, and *action*,' said Wordsworth, 'is immediate and inseparable.'[17] It is that 'Yet still' that bespeaks an enduring love and makes suffering an action, turns passive to active. Margaret is under the weight of her own troubles, and so far down that her place expresses her troubles more than her wits can now bear to; but even so there is something in her that is above these troubles, while yet she is vulnerably and commitedly immersed in them. As Arnold said of Greek tragedy, there is in this poetry 'a lofty sense of the mastery of the human spirit over its own stormiest agitations . . . a sentiment of sublime acquiescence in the course of fate, and in the dispensations of human life.'[18] 'Yet still/She loved this wretched spot' yields a 'stillness', in every sense, which takes the lines beyond irony and contradiction into a sort of tragic integrity—as if 'Yet still' was 'no longer bewildered and oppressed' by the things of the world but had 'their secret' and was 'in harmony with them'. Such poetry, says Arnold, illuminates man: 'Yet still' thus 'reconciles him with himself and the universe'.[19] At such moments Wordsworth is to Arnold the nearest thing that the nineteenth century can offer to the *complete* poet.

The lines I have chosen from the tragedy of Margaret are not unlike those touchstones of great poetry that Arnold himself singled out in 'Michael', after the father has learnt of his son's loss and cannot bring himself to complete the sheep-fold which they had begun building together:

> There is a comfort in the strength of love;
> 'Twill make a thing endurable . . .
>
> . . .—and 'tis believed by all
> That many and many a day he thither went
> And never lifted up a single stone.
>
> 'Michael' (ll. 448–66)

That '*never*' is like 'Yet still': it takes to heart the '*many and many* a day' and gets above it with a strength of love that both triumphs and weighs down, together. 'And *never* lifted up a *single* stone.' Says Arnold of this one line: 'There is nothing subtle in it, no heightening, no study of poetic style, strictly so called, at all; yet it is expression of the highest and most truly expressive kind. Nature herself seems, I say, to take the pen out of his hand, and to write for him with her own bare, sheer, penetrating power'.[20] If Wordsworth is at such moments the complete poet, he is also to Arnold almost uniquely the *natural* poet:

I remember hearing him say that 'Goethe's poetry was not

inevitable enough'. The remark is striking and true; no line in Goethe, as Goethe said himself, but its maker knew well how it came there. Wordsworth is right, Goethe's poetry is not inevitable; not inevitable enough. But Wordworth's poetry, when he is at his best, is inevitable, as inevitable as Nature herself. It might seem that Nature not only gave him the matter for his poem, but wrote his poem for him. He has no style.[21]

Yet Arnold, I have said, is an artificial and an incomplete poet. Arnold famously declared that Wordsworth's philosophical proposi-tions, however 'excellent' and 'true' in themselves, carried 'none of the characters of *poetic* truth, the kind of truth we require from a poet.'[22] But in fact it is Arnold's distance from that philosophy, in a poem such as 'The Youth of Nature', that makes a difference to Arnold's own poetry. Although Wordsworth never simply believed that universal nature existed sheerly for the sake of man, there is in Arnold's mind an emphatic break with Wordsworth and a union with Goethe when it comes to a reading of Spinoza. 'Creation,' thought Goethe, 'should be made of sterner stuff'—universal nature should rest on larger grounds than the service of man. And, says Arnold, 'More than any philosopher who has ever lived, Spinoza satisfied him here.'[23] And yet Goethe's poetry is not natural or inevitable enough! Arnold never suggests that he sees the possibility of this connection.

But Arnold's poetry tacitly does make the admission, even in bemoaning the loss of inevitability:

> The millions suffer still, and grieve,
> And what can helpers heal
> With old-world cures men half believe
> For woes they wholly feel?
>
> 'Obermann Once More' (ll. 235–6)

The last line is a deadlock and a let-down in a way that 'And never lifted up a single stone' was not. For 'wholly' is only a product of the word 'half' in the line before, and not at the command of a poet who sees life steadily and sees it whole. The poetry is so *effectively* ineffective; for we half see the problems *more* in Arnold's not being able to solve or avoid them; half see them *less* in his being their product as much as their thinker.

Wordsworth, said Arnold, has no style. But Arnold himself does have a style—a borrowed one. Again in a circle, the style is both a symptom and an expression of the disease. The disease is this:

that new authors attach themselves to the poetic expression the
founders of a literature have flowered into, which may be *learned* by
a sensitive person, to the neglect of an inward poetic life.[24]

And the poetry fills the empty inward space with feelings of its own
emptiness:

> And we have been on many thousand lines,
> And we have shown, on each, spirit and power;
> But hardly have we, for one little hour,
> Been on our own line, have we been ourselves—
> > 'The Buried Life' (ll. 57–60)

For this is not verse that can locate its own 'Buried Life'—'tracking
out our *true*, *original course*'. To Wordsworth, in particular the
Wordsworth of the 'Immortality Ode', poetry was words about one's
life which, now set in front of one's eyes, represented an effort to recall
from the back of one's mind what that life had been meant to be.
Humboldt 'was forever talking about something he called "the home
world", Wordsworthian, Platonic, before the shades of the prison
house fell.'[25] But Arnold's early poem, 'To a Gipsy Child by the
Sea-shore', turns the child of Wordsworth's 'Immortality Ode' into a
being closer to Hardy's Little Father Time in *Jude the Obscure*.[26] 'What
mood wears like complexion to thy woe?' he asks,

> Some exile's, mindful how the past was glad?
> Some angel's, in an alien planet born?
> > (ll. 25–6)

Exiled from how it should have been, living in a place not naturally
inevitable but arbitrary and alien, it is as though Arnold, in contrast to
Wordsworth, can never quite *remember* what his life was *for*; Arnold's
prime mover is more like Hardy's God than Plato's:

> For, alas, he left us each retaining
> Shreds of gifts which he refused in full.
> Still these waste us with their hopeless straining,
> Still the attempt to use them proves them null.
>
> And on earth we wander, groping, reeling;
> Powers stir in us, stir and disappear.

Ah! and he, who placed our master-feeling,
Failed to place that master-feeling clear.

'Self-Deception' (ll. 17–24)

'And each half-lives a hundred different lives.' Botched and partial incarnations make the Wordsworthian memory-word 'still' into an expression of harassment rather than endurance. 'We cannot attain to the mastery of the great artists': the 'master-feeling' remains only a feeling, unable to get out and on top of the life it exists within. 'Emotion,' said Spinoza at the end of the third part of his *Ethics*, 'is a confused idea.' By cruel half-rhymes something is rendered null in Arnold's gifts—'Still the attempt to *use* them *proves* them null'— something which, ironically, he would need even to speak of its annulment. 'Spinoza,' said Arnold, 'has made his distinction between adequate and inadequate ideas a current notion for educated Europe.' So often it is hard to know what it is that lies *beneath* a word that Arnold repeats and holds up almost as a talisman. But for once it is clear. The word 'adequate' which dominates the essay 'On the Modern Element in Literature' is Spinoza's term re-worked in the grand style, for the moral purpose of *humanizing* knowledge. In a deep sense, Arnold felt confused and inadequate.

Yet he remains lucid. For—'let us not bewilder our successors; let us transmit to them the practice of poetry . . . under which excellent works may again, perhaps, at some future time, be produced.'[27] It would, I think, have shocked Arnold to know that the successor to whom he transmits the problem of old emotions in a new age was actually Thomas Hardy. For in the poetry of memory in the nineteenth century, that is where Arnold takes his place—in between Wordsworth and Hardy, a half-and-half man again. It is not only a matter of whole poems: Arnold's 'To a Gipsy Child by the Sea-shore' becoming Hardy's 'To an Unborn Pauper Child'; 'The Youth of Nature' becoming 'Nature's Questioning'; 'Dover Beach' becoming 'The Darkling Thrush'. It is also the characteristic self-defeating nature of the lines within the poems: Arnold's 'Self-Deception',

For, alas, he left us each retaining
Shreds of gifts which he refused in full . . ., (ll. 17–18),

becomes in 'Yell'ham Wood's Story':

Life offers—to deny!

—or, in 'After the Visit',

> That which mattered most could not be.

Such lines, in Hardy as in Arnold, feel like something turned inside-out to become a blocked line of poetry: a complete view, held by one part of the poet, of the world's external system in which, for the most part, his incompleteness is frustratedly held. A masterly sense of being mastered.

Yet Arnold's positions always look lofty. Outside, After, and Above—those are his postures. Above, in a 'high place' outside Religion, he tries to salvage something from the soul within it; above, in a 'high place' outside Democracy, he seeks to supply something to life inside it. Religion and Democracy are themselves only secondary principles to him; it is what is subordinately and namelessly inside them that he is primarily concerned with. That buried life he calls Poetry. For the Idea of Poetry—as the metaphorical above the literal in which it is enclosed, as the spirit rather than the letter of the thing—stands for far more than can quite be done with it. It is as though Arnold had consciously to start from the very ends that he wanted to achieve. It is all like the poem 'Revolutions,' where God has given men the complete letters of the alphabet and they never get them in quite the right order. Somehow it always seems to come out wrong for Arnold, mis-spelling the dimly-recalled but originally-intended Word. Thus his poetry seems as he ideally wants it to be in the poem, 'Resignation', above the world; yet only on the rebound from the perception of helplessness in it. For it is only by borrowing the idea of God—in whose eye

> . . . each moment in its race,
> Crowd as we will its neutral space,
> Is but a quiet watershed
> Whence, equally, the seas of life and death are fed . . .
> 'Resignation' (ll. 257-60)

—that Arnold can temporarily achieve from above that quiet neutrality he so restlessly wanted below.

Such heights of beauty are not Hardy's—not even on 'Wessex Heights'. In Hardy's characteristic position, the potential for the view from above, with its clarity, is still trapped and held down within the very self it would transcend. It is that imprisonment of the

Wordsworthian dimension within a self fallen into mundane, personal complexities which Arnold feared and sought to avoid. But Hardy is prepared to enter the 'brazen prison' from which Arnold temporarily freed himself in order to write of it. Hardy re-inverts Arnold, turning him back down to earth and physical self:

> Arnold is wrong about provincialism, if he means anything more than a provincialism of style and manner in exposition. A certain provincialism of feeling is invaluable. It is the essence of individuality, and is largely made up of that crude enthusiasm without which no great thoughts are thought, no great deeds done.[28]

Indeed, a later poet writes thus of Hardy's willingness to start lower down:

> Perhaps one ought not to say Hardy's beliefs, but Hardy's disbeliefs; whichever term is exact, the fact is that his beliefs or disbeliefs make possible the great strength of his verse. . . . It is possible for a poet to make poetry by the direct statement of his beliefs, but it is not possible for such a poet as Hardy. The true philosophical poet is characterized by an understanding of ideas and an interest in them which absorbs his whole being. Hardy was interested in ideas, too; but predominantly in their bearing upon human life. No better characterization could be formulated than the one Hardy wrote for his novel, *Two on a Tower*: 'This slightly-built romance was the outcome of a wish to set the emotional history of two infinitesimal lives against the stupendous background of the stellar universe, and to impart to readers the sentiment that of these contrasting magnitudes the smaller might be the greater to them as men.'
>
> Hardy failed when he tried to make a direct statement of his beliefs; he succeeded when he used his beliefs to make significant the observations which concerned him. This contrast should suggest that something essential to the nature of poetry may very well be in question. . . . The minute particulars of Hardy's experience might have made a diary, history, or biography; what made them poetry was the functioning of Hardy's beliefs.[29]

—The writer is none other than the model for Humboldt, Delmore Schwartz himself. He shows how Hardy has to give up on Arnold's Dante ('the true philosophical poet'), and give up the grand style, if only to find that loss again more substantially as resisted disbelief within a diminished self. Painfully and ironically, the 'smaller might be the greater' through its own internal consciousness of its external minuteness in the universe. This is the idea quoted above from 'Resignation', its perspective turned upside-down, outside in. For with Arnold the form, even in Greek tragedy, always transcended its own content, giving 'a lofty sense of the mastery of the human spirit over its own stormiest agitations'; and even in his own poetry the honours are at least shared between the mastery above and the helplessness within the lines. But with Hardy, the form is morally and emotionally subordinate to the content which it nonetheless still physically contains and entraps. 'The Oxen' is the poem that Delmore Scwartz singles out to show how Hardy's beliefs had to turn from being liberatingly above the self to being imprisoned yet also imprisoning within it. The elders had told Hardy as a child that at twelve o'clock on Christmas Eve the very oxen knelt in their pen; no one in these (grown-up, secularized) times would now believe such a thing; 'yet', if you are Hardy, even now

> . . . I feel,
> If someone said on Christmas Eve,
>   'Come; see the oxen kneel,
>
> 'In the lonely barton by yonder coomb
>   Our childhood used to know,'
> I should go with him in the gloom,
>   Hoping it might be so.

This is provincial, not classic. Transcendent belief is reduced to and confined within the psychology of hope, and even of hoping against hope; though, within its prison, belief still has drives (childish or ancient) that can re-assume control. Nor is it that the last line is a sentimentally noble boast: on the contrary, the form of the poem seems as amazed at its own content as is Hardy at the sight of what is going on within him:

> I should go with him in the gloom
>   Hoping it might be so.

He can barely believe his belief! Form does not preside over content, it is both entrapped by and entrapping it. To Arnold this would have seemed, I think, a refusal of what form and art might stand for, as 'neutral spaces'.[30]

Hardy, said Delmore Schwartz, 'was interested in ideas, too; but predominantly in their bearing upon human life.' It is salutary to recall that for all the difference between Hardy and Arnold, Hardy's procedure as described so well by Delmore Schwartz was itself supported by—if not derived from—his reading of Arnold's essay on Wordsworth. For in his notebook Hardy copied out:

> A great poet receives his distinctive character of superiority from his application (under the conditions immutably fixed by the laws of poetic beauty and poetic truth)—from his application to his subject whatever it may be, of the ideas
> On man, on nature, and on human life,
> which he has acquired for himself.[31]

Arnold's position in between Wordsworth and Hardy is not merely historical. It is a position vital to anyone concerned with what is at stake, for poetry and for belief, between these two poets. In what seem to me the greatest lines written by anyone in the century, Arnold captures what (in retrospect) we can see it would take to turn Thomas Hardy back towards William Wordsworth, when suddenly

> A bolt is shot back somewhere in our breast
> And a lost pulse of feeling stirs again.
>   'The Buried Life' (ll. 84–5)

These lines are a touchstone and a gift.

Notes

1 'Obermann' (1869), *E in C* III (*CPW* v 300).

2 Saul Bellow, *Humboldt's Gift* (Penguin ed., 1977), 119.

3 Arnold's 'Resignation: To Fausta', ll. 209–13 (*Poems* 88). The poem is addressed to Jane, Arnold's favourite sister; the lines are Fausta's imagined thoughts.

4 Arnold's sonnet, 'Shakespeare'; the poem is quoted in *Humboldt's Gift* (ed. cit.), 122.

5 'Joubert' (1864), *E in C* I (*CPW* iii 183).

6 'Civilisation in the United States' (1888) (*CPW* xi 365).

7 Saul Bellow, *Herzog* (1964); quoted from Penguin ed. (1976), 189.

8 Preface to *Poems* 1853 (*CPW* i 15).

9 'Literature and Science' (1882); 'On Translating Homer—Last Words' (1862) (*CPW* x 68, i 188).

10 'On Translating Homer—Last Words', loc. cit. 209.

11 'The Study of Poetry' (1880), *E in C II* (*CPW* ix 174).

12 'Wordsworth' (1881), *E in C II* (*CPW* ix 51).

13 Wordsworth, *The Excursion* (1814), i ll. 87–8.

14 'Maurice de Guérin' (1863), *E in C I* (*CPW* iii 12–13).

15 Letters to Clough c. December 1847 and 1848–9 (*CL* 63, 97).

16 'Wordsworth', loc. cit. ix 51.

17 'Essay Supplementary to the Preface', *Prose Works of William Wordsworth*, ed. W. J. B. Owen and J. W. Smyser, three volumes (Oxford, 1974), iii 81.

18 Preface to *Merope* (1858) (*CPW* i 58–9).

19 'Maurice de Guérin', loc. cit. 33.

20 'Wordsworth', loc. cit. ix 53.

21 Ibid., 51–2

22 Ibid., 49.

23 'Spinoza and the Bible' (1863), *E in C I* (*CPW* iii 176).

24 Letter to Clough, late 1847 or early 1848 (*CL* 64).

25 *Humboldt's Gift*, ed. cit. 431.

26 'To a Gipsy Child by the Sea-shore' was written in 1843 or 1844. Its Stoical pessimism is a natural mood which pre-dates Arnold's formal reading of Stoical philosophers—in particular Epictetus, whom he studied in 1848. On Wordsworth's own reading of the Stoics see Jane Worthington, *Wordsworth's Reading of Roman Prose* (New Haven, Connecticut, 1946).

27 'Spinoza and the Bible', loc. cit. 181.

28 Florence Emily Hardy, *The Life of Thomas Hardy*, corrected edition (London, 1972), 146–7.

29 Delmore Schwartz, 'Poetry and Belief in Thomas Hardy', in *Hardy: A Collection of Critical Essays*, ed. A. J. Guerard, Twentieth-Century Views (Englewood Cliffs, New Jersey, 1963), 128, 130–1.

30 A comparison between, say, Arnold's 'Isolation. To Marguerite' and Hardy's 'A Broken Appointment' would show how Hardy *hardens* the form, the rhymes and repetitions, and indeed the very conflict, in order to create an aesthetic achievement which is also paid for by emotional imprisonment. Even so, there is clearly a line from Arnold through Hardy to Philip Larkin, as a comparison of 'Stanzas from the Grande Chartreuse' with Larkin's 'Church Going' would show.

31 *The Literary Notes of Thomas Hardy*, ed. L. A. Bjork (Goteberg, Sweden, 1974), vol. 1, part i (no. 1104), 122.

Empedocles and Byron Once More

BERNARD BEATTY

Nineteen eighty-eight is the bicentenary of Byron's birth as well as the centenary of Arnold's death. To bring the two figures together in this way is not merely a pious celebratory gesture, for Arnold's championing of Byron surprised many of his contemporaries, and the reasons for this admiration—as with his feeling for George Sand, which is explored elsewhere in this symposium—are perhaps still not always so readily understood as his admiration for Wordsworth and Goethe. Why did Arnold like and admire Byron so much? This is a straightforward question and, for the most part, it can receive a straightforward answer. But 'for the most part' is not quite enough. There remains something enigmatic in Arnold's response that is hard to pinpoint and understand, and yet this enigma, as so often with Arnold, seems to bring us closer to him than the clear channels of thought.

We can begin with the non-problematic. Arnold characteristically admired people who represented parts of himself as he was or would have liked to be. His admiration for the wise, retiring Joubert, for Senancour, the melancholy, post-religious seeker after consolation, for Guérin, 'elusive, undulating, impalpable,'[1] and for Lacordaire, the charismatic teacher of youth and of a nation, are some examples. It is not difficult to isolate those elements of Byron's writings and, more especially, of his personality, which spoke directly to Arnold in this way. There is Byron's persistent and passionate melancholy together with the self-protecting wit which accompanies it. There is Byron's independence of spirit. D. G. James, for instance, pointed out the importance of a phrase in Arnold's preface to his first series of *Essays in Criticism* where he writes that 'I have always sought to stand by myself'.[2] Byron clearly represented this independence on a Titanic scale. Byron's snobbery is part of this, too—his anxiety not to have the inky fingers which would mark him as a writer rather than a gentleman. At the same time, Byron, like the overworked Arnold with his regular grind in classrooms round the country, was nearly always hard up, and knew almost as well as Arnold did the drabness of English provincial life. Byron, like Arnold, was consciously European, and deplored the inward turning of English culture. He was, especially in Arnold's favourite Canto IV of *Childe Harold's Pilgrimage*, a Stoic, or a would-be or temporary Stoic. Nevertheless Byron was, as Goethe recognized,[3] a modern man who, as a liberal, ex-Calvinist aristocrat, embodied and understood that transition from feudalism to secularism hailed by Arnold as a decisive turning-point. It could not be said of him, as Arnold said of his other romantic idol Wordsworth:

> But Wordsworth's eyes avert their ken
> From half of human fate . . .
>   'Stanzas in Memory of the Author of "Obermann" ' (ll. 53–4)

On the other hand—and the mixture was part of the attraction for Arnold—Byron was disgusted by the meanness and lack of resonance of modern life. He was full of nostalgia for classical civilization and, less straightforwardly, for medieval culture.

The tension between these rival allegiances made Byron, like Arnold, a temperamental romantic who spurned romanticism in the name of a revived classicism and doubted the credentials of his own verse. Byron's first two cantos of *Childe Harold* and a translation of Horace's *De Arte Poetica* in heroic couplets, published on his return from his first Grand Tour, may be compared to Arnold's classicist preface to his 1853 volume of romantic poems. Both poets are romantics when they are defending the classics. The shifts of sensibility and attitude demanded here may be summed up in the word *mobilité*, which Lady Blessington applied to Byron[4] and which Arnold used to describe Maurice de Guérin.[5] Guérin is another figure in whom Arnold clearly recognized part of himself, and the word *mobilité* represents what he was and, to an extent, was determined to be. Byron's Titanic self-assertion protected the maze of contradictions of which, like Arnold, he was constituted.

So much is clear. So too is Arnold's admiration for those qualities which Byron possessed and he did not. Goethe, Wordsworth, and Byron indeed constitute a trio of early nineteenth-century worthies who stand in exemplary relation to the century they inaugurate, and whose sensibility and problems they understand and help to resolve. This is how they are seen, for example, in 'Memorial Verses' or in the letter to J. Dykes Campbell (22 September 1864). Here it is principally Byron's energy that Arnold admires. Gray's well-known distinction between 'black' and 'white' melancholy,[6] a distinction that Arnold fastened upon in his essay on Byron, appears to suggest some

reserve of energy as well as inhibition in black melancholy that
Arnold's own habitual white melancholy does not provoke. Where
Byron finds 'a very life in our despair,'[7] Arnold apostrophizes his own
'unquiet breast' which is 'Never by passion quite possess'd'.[8] It is the
word 'quite' here, so characteristically Arnold's, which confirms a
tone almost absurdly unlike the eerie gusto in Byron's 'very' ('a very
life in our despair'). It is easy to see why Arnold should be drawn
across the 'unlit gulph'[9] to enthusiasm for this different charge of
melancholy. He recognized and saluted it again in Emily Brontë:

> (How shall I sing her?) Whose soul
> Knew no fellow for might,
> Passion, vehemence, grief,
> Daring, since Byron died,
> That world-famed son of fire.
>
> 'Haworth Churchyard' (ll. 93–7)

Arnold himself clearly understood those extra qualities of 'passion,
vehemence, grief' that Byron possessed and he did not. It would be
odd if he did not discern other hidden compensations and balances
offered by Byron's personality. Byron, whose father died when Byron
was three, had no one to dominate and control his upbringing. He was
as fully acquainted with his id as with his superego. Byron, instead of
yearning for his buried life, could bear

> Through Europe to the Aetolian shore
> The pageant of his bleeding heart.
>
> 'Stanzas from the Grande Chartreuse' (ll. 135–6)

When these lines are repeated out of context—and Arnold has a genius
for framing repeatable phrases—they are usually presented as a criticism. That was not Arnold's original intention. The advantage does
not lie with the dumb 'kings of modern thought' who, in earlier
stanzas, grieve as much as their romantic predecessors but can only
'stand mute, and watch the waves'. It is true that Arnold is ostensibly
saying that the utterance of melancholy has not effected anything, but
the current of feeling flows with Byron (and Shelley and Senancour)
here. Arnold clearly admired the externalizing force in Byron through
which

> thousands counted every groan,
> And Europe made his woe her own . . .
>
> 'Stanzas from the Grande Chartreuse' (ll. 137–8)

Or perhaps not quite. In a letter to Clough (29 September 1848) Arnold writes:

> I have seen clean water in parts of the lake of Geneva (which whole locality is spoiled by the omnipresence there of that furiously flaring bethiefed rushlight the vulgar Byron) . . . (*CL* 92)

Here, 'The pageant of his bleeding heart' appears as something 'vulgar' and 'furiously flaring', and the 'world-famed son of fire' has dwindled to a 'rushlight'. We may deduce therefore that there is an undertone, a hostile latency, in Arnold's famous line about Byron's 'bleeding heart', much as Blake's *Songs of Innocence* may be read from their own standpoint or from that of the 'experience' which they deny but which is latent in them.

It might be thought possible and useful to try to pin down Arnold's ambivalence about Byron either in relation to the development of Arnold's thought or to some fundamental differences in emphasis. Something along these lines can be done. William A. Jamison, for example, summarizes it thus:

> The development of Arnold's view of Byron—from boyish enthusiasm for the Byronic to youthful distaste for the vulgarity of the man and the looseness of his art to mature admiration for the passionate rebel—parallels roughly the vicissitudes of Byron's reputation during the century.[10]

Similarly we could take Arnold's distinction between Byron's inability (as Arnold saw it) to teach us and his power to move:

> He taught us little; but our soul
> Had *felt* him like the thunder's roll.
>
> 'Memorial Verses' (ll. 8–9)

We can at once place this verse of 1850 with the major distinction of the 1881 preface to Arnold's selection from Byron, which seems to re-affirm the same point:

On the other hand, this splendid personality and unmatched talent, this unique Byron, 'is quite too much in the dark about himself'; nay, 'the moment he begins to reflect he is a child'.[11]

Arnold's version of Goethe's critique is entirely consistent with his earlier view. What more is there to say?

It cannot, however, be quite as straightforward as this. After all, Arnold's abuse of Byron in the 1848 letter to Clough occurs only two years before the apparently heartfelt encomium in 'Memorial Verses' (1810). If we continue the quotation already given from 'Memorial Verses', we read:

> With shivering heart the strife we saw
> Of passion with eternal law;
> And yet with reverential awe
> We watch'd the fount of fiery life
> Which serv'd for that Titanic strife. (ll. 10–14)

How can we have 'reverential awe' for a 'furiously flaring bethiefed rushlight'? The distinction between teaching and feeling will not help us at all because Arnold's objection to Byron in the letter to Clough is to the inferior quality of Byron's feelings, not to deficiencies in his thought. Arnold is looking at the same properties, ridiculing them as a 'rushlight' and reverencing them as a 'fount of fiery life'.

We should, perhaps, approach this problem from another direction. Arnold's wonderful choice of the word 'pageant' for Byron's wounded, self-articulating progress across Europe indicates a disturbance in Arnold's own sensibility rather than a distinction in his mind. Arnold could not decide, it would seem, whether his own ironical and fastidious disaffection with the world about him found its Titanic exemplar in Byron or whether Byron vulgarized that detachment or, perhaps, managed also some immersion in the world that made Arnold recognize his own impulse to 'plunge deeper in the bowering wood'[12] as mere impotence. Arnold's distinction between what Byron 'taught us' and what 'our soul / Had felt' through him is not unreal, but it represents, as the later use of Goethe's distinction does on a larger scale, a rationalization of a divergence which Arnold could not wholly comprehend. Arnold's famous distinctions, manifestly, are not analytic like those of St Thomas Aquinas or Kant or Newman— that is, they are not clarifications which will lead to further insight— but are rather rhetorically based judgements which secure the poise of the writer. Arnold appears simultaneously to celebrate and exorcize the spirit of Byron in an equipoise which remains essentially unchanged throughout his life.

There is therefore something enigmatic about the relationship between the two poets. We cannot solve an enigma without stating it and, once stated, an enigma, be it the sphinx's or Turandot's, is well on the way to solution. We can indicate something of its nature by reverting to Arnold's essay on Gray. There is nothing in the least puzzling about Arnold's sympathetic understanding of Gray. The phrase used of Gray by James Brown, Master of Pembroke College, 'He never spoke out', is a leitmotiv in the essay.[13] It represents all of Gray and, again, an important facet of Arnold himself. In the same way, when we read Arnold's characteristic attempt to explain Gray's 'sterility' by asserting that 'Gray, a born poet, fell upon an age of prose',[14] we will inevitably apply the remark to Arnold himself with the additional twist that Arnold, 'a born poet', deliberately sought out a life of prose from at least 1857, when he became, albeit temporarily, a professor like Gray. But Byron did 'speak out', and he is a prototype for that other Arnold who admired Byron's speaking out, spoke out himself, and was excited by doing so:

> It is very animating to think that at last one has a chance of *getting at* the English public.[15]

The weapons chosen here in 1863 are 'the power of *persuasion*, of *charm*', and the medium is prose. It is not a Byronic mix, though Byron can, on occasion, charm, persuade, write good prose, and get at the English public. This is exactly the problem. It is easy to see how Byron could be the prototype for so many of Arnold's projected values and undertakings, but it is much harder to see how in fact he is so. There is a gap between Arnold's sustained admiration for Byron, his frequent reference to him, his imitation in his youth of Byron's verse and manner, his critical elevation in his old age of Byron as the greatest poet with Wordsworth of the nineteenth century and, on the other hand, that want of connection with—almost, it seems, of real interest in—Byron's poems and concerns. Take, for instance, the case of *Empedocles on Etna*.

Empedocles on Etna is often adduced as, in some sense, Byronic and, with respect to form, at least, bears a resemblance to Byron's *Manfred*. It is, apart from *Alaric at Rome*, the most obvious example of Byron's influence on Arnold. Both plays are dramatic poems which culminate in the death of their proud, distraught, but vociferous heroes. *Manfred* has more characters, but the contrast of Manfred with the Chamois Hunter and the Abbott roughly corresponds to that of Empedocles with Pausanias and Callicles. Metaphors of height and references to ageing are central to both. Manfred soliloquizes on the Jungfrau; Empedocles on Etna. Manfred explains that he is vastly older than his chronological age; Empedocles dramatizes human life at emblematic dawn, noon, and night. Both Manfred and Empedocles are superior to their fellows but find spiritual aridity in their elevation. Both plays distinguish the disengaging habits of later knowledge from the instinctive associations of early life. Rest and repose are key words in both. We could enlarge on these parallels and, doubtless, unearth others. But if Arnold did recall *Manfred*, he would seem to have done so only in the sense that he recalled Wordsworth in 'Resignation'. Kenneth Allott once characterized 'Resignation' wryly and exactly as a poem,

> in which Arnold seems to have remembered some of Wordsworth's ideas for the purpose of disagreeing with them.[16]

Perhaps even this is to overstate the case. Did Arnold recall Byron's ideas at all, even if to disagree with them? If we state Byron's major concerns, as they are so characteristically expressed in *Manfred*, it comes as something of a surprise to see how wholly uninterested Matthew Arnold was in any of them at any time.

Much of Byron's poetry is concerned with transgressors (pirates, outlaws, renegades, violators of sexual codes) who, though guilty, proclaim their moral superiority and yet, invariably, find punishment. Doubtless these characters can be rationalized, as Goethe rationalized *Cain*, by being seen as instances of sensibilities in transition between old and new moral codes, and thus as intimations of Arnold's 'modern spirit' which seeks to remove the 'want of correspondence' between 'accredited dogmas, customs, rules' and 'modern times'.[17] The fact remains that Byron is obsessed with crime and punishment. Arnold is not interested in either. Manfred is a metaphysical criminal. Arnold sees him as a rebel without a cause who has some severe psychological problems:

> And all Byron's heroes, not so much in collision with outward things, as breaking on some rock of revolt and misery in the depths of their own nature; Manfred, self-consumed, fighting blindly and passionately with I know not what, having nothing of the consistent development and intelligible motive of Faust[18]

The image of 'breaking on some rock of revolt' is implied again and again in Arnold's references to Byron. But in fact, whatever *Manfred* is about, it cannot be about 'breaking on some rock of revolt'. Manfred's last line,

Old man! 'tis not so difficult to die.[19]

was, Byron insisted, the most important line in the play.[20] It indicates some form of acquiescence in Manfred towards which he and the whole play move. Byron's play opens, as Arnold's closes, with a suicide scene, but Manfred is led, humiliated, from that scene. The play pivots between Manfred's wished-for death and the death which comes to him.

Arnold did not see *Manfred* in this way because, as a critic of literature, his interest in process was of a different order. Of course, he was aware of process in his own life but there was, as R. Peter Burnham has argued, a 'natural Platonism' in his temperament which resisted finding value in anything that changed.[21] On the one hand, 'natural magic' and feeling, on the other, fine phrasing, judicious teaching and, in deliberate contrast, heroic action, were what he looked for and what he found. Byron's poetry did not 'teach' us anything, but was '*felt*'. It is curiously revealing, then, that Arnold should have admired Wordsworth's and Byron's poetry so deeply since the force and character of their writing are so much bound up with process. Arnold's two volumes of selections from Wordsworth and Byron almost seem designed to take the process out of the poetry. Manfred's death scene does in fact form one of Arnold's selected passages, but no longer ends a play which we interpret via its close. Like many of his contemporaries, Arnold had a penchant for death scenes. He selected a disproportionate number of them from Byron's poetry, and he includes the dying speech of the Doge Marino Faliero, which he had recited publicly at Winchester nearly half a century before. The keynote of the Doge's speech is defiant energy, and Manfred is not without this, but he does not end up 'breaking on some rock of revolt' with defiant energy for, in the closing lines, such energy has been transmuted to an eerie quietness. Byron, I think, is trying to dramatize an almost imperceptible transition between defiance and acquiescence (not 'resignation') which lies at the centre of his own understanding and of his art. By the time he was writing the final cantos of *Don Juan*, Byron was prepared or almost prepared to accept the vocabulary of orthodox Christianity for this transition. But at the time of writing *Manfred* (1816-17), it was important both to suggest this vocabulary and to repudiate it. Hence, in the third act of the play, the centrality of the Abbott, whose counsel is clearly rejected but whose hand Manfred asks for and clasps as he dies. We might call this 'cold humility'. Manfred comes to something like humility, but is at pains to distance himself from the hot humility 'which is the fascination of saints and good men'. This wonderful distinction comes from G. K. Chesterton who coined it specifically for Matthew Arnold.[22] Chesterton argued that Arnold has a certain kind of humility, exemplary so far as it went, and especially so because Arnold 'was not naturally a humble man; he might even be called a supercilious one'. Nevertheless, humility 'was with Arnold a mental need'.[23] And, we might add, it is a need of Empedocles, too, 'for whose hurt courage is not the cure' (II i 14).

As soon as we state the similarity, however, we mark the difference between Manfred and Empedocles. In *Manfred* we cannot avoid noticing how the play both vindicates and rebukes Manfred's pride and reveals him in a different position at the end than he was at the beginning. The play is confusing, but the focus is clear. *Empedocles*, on the other hand, is much more tightly structured but more unfocused. We can explain this by recalling how Byron intensified certain aspects of himself in Manfred in order to defend and objectify these features but also to counter them and move beyond them. And this is what happened. Tennyson did something similar in *Maud*. But Arnold never projects himself as directly as this in his poetry. His lyric voice is not a projection in this sense at all. We can see him doing something analogous to Byron, however, in his portraits of other writers such as Joubert, Guérin, Gray, and Senacour, in whom a distinctively feminine diffidence is marked. Senacour is a special case because he has already projected himself as Obermann just as Byron has in Harold or *Manfred*. Yet Arnold is never quite objectifying himself in these portraits. They are apparently someone else. Writing them allows him to preserve his private self, though covertly. It is through them that he keeps faith with the melancholy that characterizes all his poetry. In the same measure, Arnold maintains his apparent repudiation of the self revealed in these poems because he treats the self as *un autre* and refuses to assist its transformation by wholly articulating it. Wordsworth and Byron, in ways very different from each other, did the exact opposite of this, which may form part of their secret attraction for Arnold, but probably does not. Arnold never stands to Byron in the openly envious relation that Coleridge stood to Wordsworth.

In *Empedocles on Etna* Arnold comes near to a Byronic complex of ideas, but something interposes. If we read 'The Scholar-Gipsy', for example, the way in which formal elements of Gray, Keats, Milton, and Shelley are woven together is manifest and uncomplicated, though dextrous and pleasing (the underlying dissensions from Keats, frequently remarked upon, are another matter, pointing once more to characteristic ambiguities). The 'Scholar-Gipsy', as a poetic device recalling Keats's use of his nightingale or Shelley's use of his skylark, served Arnold's purpose by representing his own apparent desire for transformation whilst confirming his luxuriating obduracy of will and scrupulously maintained enervation. The distance maintained between the 'I' or 'We' of the poet and his fellow 'half-believers' and the 'He' and 'Thou' of the Scholar-Gipsy is a strategy, covertly assisted by the Keatsian abundance of detail, which makes of 'this strange disease of modern life' the Gipsy's own relished and enchanted ground. Arnold, like Keats, would rather live within the rare stability of a divided life than be Wordsworth or Byron and live at that point where energy flows in transformation. In *Empedocles* he comes closest to questioning this position, for humility 'was with Arnold a mental need'. But wherever Byron is in the poem, he will not be so readily discerned as Gray, Keats, Milton, and Shelley can be in 'The Scholar-Gipsy'.

We can begin with some agreed simplifications. *Empedocles on Etna* endorses Empedocles's version of Goethe's and Arnold's own wisdom, expressed in the conclusion to his long speech in Act I:

> Nurse no extravagant hope;
> Because thou must not dream, thou need'st not then despair!
>
> (I ii 425–6)

However, we set two markers against Empedocles's wisdom. The first is Callicles (Byron might have made him a woman). The second is Empedocles's suicide and the wholly different speech which precedes it. Empedocles appears no more able to live by his wisdom than the Stoic in Johnson's *Rasselas*. Arnold himself, of course, makes exactly this point in his letter to Henry Dunn (12 November 1867). Through Callicles, we are shown a different tenor of life. Callicles also has the best and the last lines in the play.

What are we to make of this? The most available courses are to read the play unbiographically as an expression of negative capability or understand it as a dramatized version of Arnold's intellectual doubts and earnestness, lyric pain and joy. These voices do not confront one another directly as Lamia and Apollonius do in Keats's *Lamia*. Instead, Arnold separates and juxtaposes Empedocles and Callicles in almost operatic fashion. There is, nevertheless, one point where they interact. At the beginning of Act II, Empedocles 'advances to the edge of the crater' whilst Callicles 'is heard below singing'. Callicles's song celebrates the universal appeal of the lyre's voice with the exception of Typho, who lies punished and buried under the volcano and, in Callicles's mythical thinking, *is* the volcano. This is of a piece with final song, where he says of Etna:

> Not here, O Apollo!
> Are haunts meet for thee. (II i 421–2)

It is as though poetry can handle everything except the unreachable, still-willed energies of pain trapped in the hearts of things, and with Empedocles's 'lonely thinking-power' (II i 376), which ascends in order to plunge into them.

Empedocles takes up Callicles's song about Typho's punishment by Jove and re-interprets it as an instance of the repression of 'The brave, impetuous heart' by 'the subtle, contriving head' (II i 90–1).[24] If we recall Callicles's long account in song of Marsyas' punishment for hubris (II i 125–90) and Empedocles's own reference to Apollo's slaying of Pytho (II i 205), then we seem to have a densely Byronic complex. Intellectualized defiance of gods and received opinion, elemental energy, and a punishment of both which is mean-spirited and yet the foundation of song, characterize both this aspect of *Empedocles* and much of Byron's poetry. This is how Shelley dramatizes Byron in 'Julian and Maddalo'. If we note that the lyrical element (Callicles, Astarte) was once acknowledged by Empedocles and Manfred, though they are subsequently shut off from it, then the correspondence seems exact.

However, 'this aspect of *Empedocles*' is not the same thing as *Empedocles*. It is not so much that the play as a whole contains more than these concerns; rather, they do not constitute its centre, for Arnold does not allow the poem to have a centre. The idea of punishment with all its ambiguities is not carried through. Attention shifts instead to Empedocles' inability to live in society or in solitude, then to the contrast between youth and age, and then to the mind's persistence. When Byron depicts suicide, as for example in his magnificent account of Christian Fletcher's suicide in *The Island*, the suicide comes out of the life which insists upon this conclusion. So it does with

Empedocles, but only up to a point. There is some gap between
Empedocles's lucidity and his self-destructiveness. Anyone who reads
the play for the first time is surprised by Empedocles's death when it
occurs, despite the fact that we have been expecting nothing else from
the outset of the play. Empedocles appears to snatch a moment when
he can plunge into the crater as though the moment chosen depends on
the surface flow of his impressions:

> Leap and roar, thou sea of fire!
> My soul glows to meet you.
> Ere it flag, ere the mists
> Of despondency and gloom
> Rush over it again,
> Receive, save me!

(II i 411–16)

Byron would here have given us grandeur, pathos, sardonic humour,
glee, or an intelligible context for an *acte gratuit*, as in *Cain*. Arnold
avoids all of these. If we want to understand Empedocles's suicide and
its timing, it is no use re-reading his final speech in hopes of extracting
some intellectual, dramatic, or emotional logic which will explain it.
What we can do instead, rather fashionably as it turns out, is to attend
to the gaps in Empedocles's peroration. There is one 'long pause', a
further 'long silence', and then a shorter 'pause' followed by two sets
of dots indicating unanswered questions, in the play's final section.
Arnold clearly intends a striking contrast with Empedocles's lengthy,
uninterrupted, and remarkably coherent speech in stanzas, accompanied by his own harp, in Act I. That speech is followed by 'a long
pause' before Callicles sings the story of Cadmus and Harmonia.
Empedocles's first speech is framed by silence, and the silence between
each of its stanzas (only one of which is fully enjambed) imparts
harmony, cogency, and authority to his utterance. In his final speech
in Miltonic free verse, however, the scattered pauses threaten the
utterance, disclose the unlit gulph from which it springs, and explain
its sudden shifts and inconsistencies. The carefully edited harmony of
Callicles's final song comes, manifestly, from somewhere else.

Yet Arnold chose Empedocles as his subject. He talked of completing
a poem about Lucretius, another religionless philosopher, but he never
did so. He chose instead the philosopher who plunged into a volcano
and he dramatized that event without fully explicating it. The most
crucial speech in the play is as much made up of the long silences and

gaps which interrupt it as it is of articulated pattern. In Empedocles himself we have a Byronic figure who, nevertheless, plays *Manfred* in reverse and makes us 'feel our powers of effort flag' (II i 387) as no Byronic hero does. This is no very edifying yield, but it is distinct and real.

My argument is in the nature of an hypothesis which will clarify the enigma of the gaps in Empedocles's speech, the gap between Empedocles and Callicles, and Arnold's extraordinary reverence for (or need of) Byron despite his often patronizing relationship and apparent indifference to his concerns. If we look back to Arnold's account of Manfred in 'On the Study of Celtic Literature', we find it preceded by a quotation from one of Byron's late lyrics:

> There is the Titanism of the Celt, his passionate, turbulent, indomitable reaction against the despotism of fact; and of whom does it remind us so much as of Byron?
>> The fire which on my bosom preys
>> Is lone as some volcanic isle;
>> No torch is kindled at its blaze;
>>> A funeral pile![25]

Well, as a matter of fact (and fact is the matter here), it does not remind me of 'the Titanism of the Celt' or the lament of Llywarch Hen with which Arnold compares it. And, as it happens, the context tells against Arnold's insistence. The opening lines of the poem:

> 'Tis time this heart should be unmoved,
>> Since others it hath ceased to move:
> Yet though I cannot be beloved,
>> Still let me love!

do not reveal a 'reaction against the despotism of fact' but dramatize a tension between Byron's impulse to love (Llywarch Hen bemoans the fact that he has lost it), his beloved's lack of interest in him, and the appropriateness of accepting this at his age. All this is then turned on its head by Byron's dramatic rejection.

In *Empedocles*, Arnold moves from his usual elegiac landscape and, instead, juxtaposes fertile valley with bare volcanic mountain, produces a sage who talks like Goethe and feels like Arnold, and finally throws him into the heart of Byron's magnificent, buried, but almost ridiculously eruptive life. Callicles, meanwhile, sings some myths below and thus performs the healing functions of Wordsworth's art, but for whom exactly is not quite clear. If we are going to make recognitions in *Empedocles* like those so visible in 'The Scholar-Gipsy', then the interpretation will turn out something like this. It is the point at which Byron is recognized that is significant. Leon Gottfried suggested in passing that Byron was 'a shadow or submerged image' in Arnold's poetry.[26] So he was. Byron was the buried Titan life, 'the soul's subterranean depth'[27] who substantiated and defended the restless misery personified in Empedocles. Senancour and Guérin, even Gray and Leopardi, are fellow exemplars too tinged with pathos and too deficient in scale to perform this task. Wordsworth and Goethe have neither of these deficiencies, but in effect accuse Arnold of failing to be healed and animated by Nature or an updated Stoicism. Wordsworth therefore has, in Arnold's version of cultural history, refused to come to terms with the Modern Spirit, and Goethe, who articulates the Modern Spirit, proffers a wisdom that Empedocles cannot finally live by. Only Byron offers the spectacle of a Titanic restlessness on so large a scale that it cannot be derided, and which Arnold can hail as distinctively modern. If Arnold is right about Byron, then Arnold's own melancholy gift of poetry, insistent self-will, and inexplicable pain are vindicated by volcanic under-sources and explained by the peculiar condition of modern life. He is both Celt and modern man. Byron defends this mixture against all who challenge it, makes it attractive, and at the same time reveals it to be quite appalling. Arnold is excited by this recognition throughout his life because it is always his own life that he sees in it.

We might say that the cult of Byron is, from the beginning, a condition of Arnold's own self-recognition. Byron is the shadow-self who justifies Arnold's self-determination ('I have always sought to stand by myself'). Of course Arnold does not think that he is Byron. Byron simply safeguards the most vulnerable and precious elements in Arnold's personality, about which he is both proud and shy. We are not meant to understand all of this. Arnold did not want an official biography, and advised his sister in a famous letter[28] (1849) not to 'make my poems square in all their parts' because 'I am fragments'. Yet in *Empedocles*, perhaps out of cold humility, Arnold produced a poem which, though it does not quite add up, gives away Arnold's unByronic reasons for placing a premium on the Byronic. Indeed the fact that it does not quite add up reveals these hidden reasons to us, just as the gaps and silences in Empedocles's final speech direct us away from a coherent interpretation of his words as sufficient explanation for his suicide.

Byron's energy in defiance forms an indispensable substratum in Arnold's difficult poise. For this reason, he will always give Byron the highest praise whilst, with most of the other vocabularies at his disposal, diminishing his status. In this case, at any rate, Arnold's disinterested criticism is profoundly (or subterraneanly) partisan in its origins.

Notes

[1] 'Maurice de Guérin' (1863), *E in C I* (*CPW* iii 230).

[2] Preface, *E in C I* (*CPW* iii 287; quoted by D. G. James in *Matthew Arnold and the Decline of English Romanticism* (Oxford, 1951), 11.

[3] *Conversations with Eckermann*, ed. J. K. Moorhead, trans. J. Oxenford (London, 1930), 211.

[4] Leslie A. Marchand, *Byron, A Portrait* (London, 1971); quoted from the 1976 paperback edition, 399.

[5] 'Maurice de Guérin', loc. cit. 17.

[6] Letter of 27 May 1742, *The Letters of Thomas Gray*, ed. D. C. Tovey (London, 1909), i 102.

[7] Byron, *Childe Harold's Pilgrimage* III xxxiv.

[8] 'A Summer Night', 1. 32 (*Poems* 282).

[9] 'The Youth of Nature', 1. 102 (*Poems* 258).

[10] William A. Jamison, *Arnold and the Romantics* (Copenhagen, 1958), 58.

[11] 'Byron' (1881), *E in C 11* (*CPW* ix 228).

[12] 'The Scholar-Gipsy', 1. 207 (*Poems* 355).

[13] 'Thomas Gray' (1880), *E in C II* (*CPW* ix 189–204).

[14] Ibid., 200.

[15] Letter to his mother, 29 October 1863 (*Letters* i 201).

[16] Kenneth Allott, 'Matthew Arnold', in *The Victorians*, ed. Arthur Pollard (London, 1969), 48; see also his discussion of Arnold and *Manfred* in *N&Q* n.s. ix (1962), 300–3.

[17] 'Heinrich Heine' (1863), *E in C I* (*CPW* iii 109).

[18] *The Study of Celtic Literature* (1867), lecture vi (*CPW* iii 373).

[19] *Manfred* III iv 151.

[20] See *The Works of Lord Byron*, ed. E. H. Coleridge (London, 1898–1906) iv 136n.1.

—

21 See Peter Burnham, ' "Empedocles on Etna" and Matthew Arnold's Argument with History', in *The Arnoldian* (vol. 12, no. 2, fall 1984; 1–21).

22 G. K. Chesterton, 'Matthew Arnold', *Essays Literary and Critical* (London, 1906), ix.

23 Ibid., 372.

24 'Empedocles misinterprets the song', asserts Paul Zietlow in a stimulating article which traces some of the ironies in the poem's references to Typho. See his 'Heard but Unheeded: The Songs of Callicles in Matthew Arnold's *Empedocles on Etna*' in *VP* (vol. 21, no. 3, autumn 1983; 243). See also Ruth apRoberts's account of Callicles and Typho in 'The Future of Poetry is Immense' in *The Arnoldian* (vol. 4, no. 1, fall 1976).

25 *The Study of Celtic Literature*, loc. cit. 372.

26 Leon Gottfried, *Matthew Arnold and the Romantics* (London, 1963), 76.

27 'The Buried Life', l. 73 (*Poems* 286).

28 Letter to his sister Jane, March 1849, *Unpublished Letters*, ed. Arnold Whitridge (New Haven, 1923), 18.

Matthew Arnold and George Sand

RUTH APROBERTS

Predictions are always a dangerous game. Matthew Arnold hazarded one in 1887: George Sand is now, he acknowledged, in eclipse, having given way to the realists: the mere 'curiosity' of Balzac, the 'severe and pitiless truth' of Flaubert and Zola;[1] but, as he said when a statue was raised to her at La Châtre in 1884, in a hundred years George Sand and her master Rousseau 'will have established their superiority to Balzac.'[2] If you paused to look about you in 1984, you would not have seen a definitive shifting in the ranks of the novelists, but you would have seen Rousseau standing pretty secure; he remains challenging, as a thinker, an influence, and an artist. And you would have certainly seen a veritable flood of new works in print about George Sand, if not a definitive change in rank.

A good number of these recent publications on George Sand are in response to new feminist interests. One might, I suppose, make a study of Arnold in respect of feminism; and yet I think it not a very rewarding line. I do not remember his making any pronouncements on the subject. One hears, at times, the note of male chauvinism, in his remarks on Harriet Martineau ('what an unpleasant life and unpleasant nature'), Margaret Fuller ('brazen female . . . what rot did she and the other female dogs of Boston talk'). Charlotte Brontë ('a fire without aliment—one of the most distressing barren sights'), and even the inoffensive Harriet Beecher Stowe ('a gorgon').[3] But when it came to intellectual women he liked, there was no condescension as to a mere female: his mother, his sister K[4], Lady de Rothschild. And his unstinting admiration went out to the actress Rachel, and to his only female literary subjects, Eugénie de Guérin—and George Sand. Sand, however, is uniquely honored by him: she is the only woman writer quoted to any extent in his *Note-Books*, and virtually the only novelist. In his writings on her, he shows himself troubled by her sexual freedom but not, I think, by her feminism. The feminism is in fact only one aspect of her consistent gospel of social equality as the enactment of the New Testament *amour*, or charity, and the coming realization of God on earth. I think finally it is the consistency of her vision and its encompassing religious fervency that held Arnold's devotion. Trilling is right when he observes: 'she fired his youth, she fortified his age.'[5] Patricia Thomson has shown how very widely she was read and admired in England, by Jane Welsh Carlyle, Elizabeth Barrett, the Brontës, George Eliot and George Henry Lewes, and then later by Thomas Hardy and Henry James. But Arnold is her most particular champion, and while her influence on his poetry has been fairly well explored, I think I can show evidence of a deeper sympathy in a religious like-mindedness that suffuses all his work, poetry and prose alike.

At Oxford, the young Arnold-Clough-Walrond 'set' took her up enthusiastically. She was fashionable—a minority cult figure. Yet it was much to their credit that they chose this particular strain of romantic idealism, marked by such adventurous and astonishing intelligence. Arnold's enthusiasm was such that he made a pilgrimage to see her in remote Nohant, and as is well known, she told Renan (who later told John Morley who told Arnold) that he gave her the impression of 'un Milton, jeune et voyageant.' She in turn impressed him with her frankness and ease, her 'simplicity,' and he records that she poured out tea for him, that '*boisson fade et mélancolique*, as Balzac called it.'[6] Patricia Thomson has an amusing correction: the phrase was not Balzac's but George Sand's own, from *L'Homme de neige*![7] He was more influenced by her than he knew. In 1877, in his commemorative essay written for her death on 8 June 1876, he looks back on those enchanted 'days of *Valentine*, days of *Lélia*, days never to return! . . . how ineffaceable is their impression! How the sentences . . . still linger in our memory and haunt the ear with their cadences!'[8] It was not George Sand alone; she is closely connected for him with other important influences—Senancour and the de Guérins, and later Sainte-Beuve and Renan. She herself read Senancour's *Obermann* at the suggestion of Sainte-Beuve, and Obermann became for her as for Arnold a tutelary spirit of those years. Her *Lélia* was called at the time 'the cry of un Obermann féminisé'.[9] She recommended Maurice de Guérin to Arnold, either in person, as Iris Sells fancies,[10] or by her preface to *Le Centaure*, the poem which so enchanted Arnold and occasioned a memorable essay.[11]

It is surprising at first to find how often the Victorians, Arnold included, connect George Sand with Goethe. But the similarity, once suggested, is indeed striking. There is the rather alarming sexual freedom, a great, devouring largeness of mind, a huge creative energy, a continual *development* in its Victorian sense of *Bildung*, the liberation from conventional religion coupled with a deeply 'religious' spirit, and an enormous capacity for work. Even Carlyle, who first hated her without reading her, set to work to read and indict her, but failed, and acknowledged 'there is something Goethean about the woman.'[12] Arnold's niece Mary Ward writes of Sand's *Consuelo* and Goethe's *Wilhelm Meister* as exercising similar 'liberating and enchanting' powers.[13] Arnold writes, 'the hour of agony and revolt passed away for George Sand, as it passed away for Goethe, as it passes away for their readers likewise', but, he concludes, George Sand's early works can no more be forgotten than *Werther*.[14]

In his essay of 1877, he tells how the English public generally think of her as a story-teller, a novelist, but argues that she is more than that, 'more than a maker of charming stories . . . more than a creator of characters.'[15] The only other time he takes a novelist for a subject is in the case of Tolstoi, in 1887, and he explains in a letter of the following year why he breaks the rule: Tolstoi also is more than a novelist, 'because of Tolstoi's religious ideas.'[16] And in the George Sand essay, the religious ideas come to the fore; Arnold describes them and quotes them at length because they are really his own.

> Her religion connected itself with this ideal [of social new-birth]. In the convent where she was brought up, she had in youth had an awakening of fervent mystical piety in the Catholic form. That form she could not keep. Popular religion of all kinds, with its deep internal impossibilities, its 'heaven and hell serving to cover the illogical manifestations of the Divinity's apparent designs respecting us,' its 'God made in our image, silly and malicious, vain and puerile, irritable or tender, after our fashion,' lost all sort of hold upon her:—
>
> 'Communion with such a God is impossible to me; I confess it. He is wiped out from my memory: there is no corner where I can find him any more. Nor do I find such a God out of doors either; he is not in the fields and waters, he is not in the starry sky. No, nor yet in the churches where men bow themselves; it is an extinct message, a dead letter, a thought that has done its day. Nothing of his belief, nothing of this God, subsists in me any longer.'
>
> She refused to lament over the loss, to esteem it other than a benefit:—
>
> 'It is an addition to our stock of light, this detachment from the idolatrous conception of religion.'[17]

He discerns three 'principal elements' in her career: 'the cry of agony and revolt, the trust in nature and beauty, the aspiration toward a purged and renewed human society.'[18] This tripartite analysis represents, it is important to note, a *development*. Alexis in Sand's novel, *Spiridion*, is a man characterized by his movement through *phases*. So also was Goethe; he believed in going through *phases* and in the doctrine of perpetual growth, or *Bildung*. So also did George Sand, and so also did Matthew Arnold. And the shape of Arnold's development is the shape of Sand's. 'The cry of agony and revolt' is Goethe's *Werther*, Sand's *Lélia*, Arnold's 'Obermann', *Empedocles on Etna*, and 'Dover Beach'. 'The trust in nature' evolved in Sand's nature ecstasies in *Spiridion*, *Valentine*, and the later *romans champêtres*, *François le Champi*, *Jeanne*, *La Mare au Diable*, *Les Maitres sonneurs*. In Arnold, it is Callicles's songs and 'Lines written in Kensington Gardens' ('In my helpless cradle I/Was breathed on by the rural Pan'). It is in the Wordsworthian elements running through all his life: his careful reports in letters of the first spring flowers, his rest 'in the flowery lap of earth'. George Sand is in fact often compared to Wordsworth both for her feeling for nature and her feeling for those common country people living close to it. (The *Zeitgeist* was to see to it that the humble folk in the verse tales of Crabbe and Wordsworth were to come into their own in the greater spaciousness and chiaroscuro of the novel, in Sand, and in Hardy, who borrowed much from Sand.) Sand's 'trust in beauty' is her good faith in the arts: her novels are remarkable for going by turns with marvellous expertise into music of various kinds, acting, mosaic-work, portrait painting, landscape painting—and literature. 'She invented an art-literature,' said Oscar Wilde.[19] For Arnold, the 'trust in beauty' is his abiding faith in the power of 'poetry,' and his body of criticism, executed in that faith. 'The aspiration toward a purged and renewed human society' informs all her later works, and the same aspiration is expressed in Arnold's vision of '*One common wave of thought and joy/Lifting mankind again!*'[20] It is the motive for his whole body of social, political, and religious writings. And so he discerns in Sand a very sympathetic parallel to the course of his own career.

'Enough—and more than enough—has been written on George Sand's love affairs'—this is the way Patricia Thomson begins her fine study of Sand's literary influence in England. Now the *Zeitgeist* turns in a different direction and cultivates a general interest in religious matters; a recent French study by Henri Bourdet-Guillerault concentrates not on the love affairs or the literary career, but the religion.[21] The author tells how he used to see in her 'nothing but a passionate, romantic love, no longer even counting her lovers, and accordingly absolutely a stranger to religion'. But he discovers 'one who lived in the light of a faith which though not of the most orthodox was none the less profound.'[22] 'Her nature was primordially and essentially religious.'[23] He traces her early fervent religious experiences in the convent school, her search for a spiritual leader, her discipleship to Lamennais whose retreat Arnold describes so sympathetically in his essay on Maurice de Guérin, Lamennais's view of a Christianity larger than Roman Catholicism, and his Christian socialism; she turns from him to Pierre Leroux, who was more activist and more political, and convinced that Christianity was itself too limited. He saw Christianity as a stage in the development toward socialism and equality, by creative evolution. George Sand kept this ideal before her. Actually, Bourdet-Guillerault's whole book is an expansion of the few pages Arnold devotes to her religion, and is quite in accord with his analysis. Arnold quotes her on 'Le sentiment de la vie idéale, qui n'est autre que la vie normale telle que nous sommes appelés à la connaître,' and he translates: 'The sentiment of the ideal life, which is none other than man's normal life as we shall some day know it.'[24] When he makes his important political statement in 'Equality', he quotes her: 'The human ideal, as well as the social ideal, is to achieve equality.' Equality is 'the goal of man and the law of the future.'[25] The political goal is the enactment of her religion.

One of her novels is particularly shaped by the teachings of Lamennais and Leroux: *Spiridion*, 1842.[26] It is full of visions and mystic experiences and nightmares, and has an absolute dearth of sexual interest. Even many devoted Sandists have found it heavy going. It may pretty safely be presumed that Arnold read it when it was new, as he read everything else of hers. But in 1882 he was re-reading it and included no less than thirty extracts from it in his *Note-Books* for that year.[27] Arnoldians at least might be interested in reading this peculiar novel. The book was also a favourite of Renan's, that other French writer to whom Arnold was intellectually very close. There is one excellent little learned book about it: Jean Pommier's *George Sand et le rêve monastique*: '*Spiridion*.'[28] The title serves to remind us that Arnold too had a *rêve monastique*, a monastic dream: 'Stanzas from the Grande Chartreuse'. It seems to me that there are overtones in it from *Spiridion*. '*What dost thou in this living tomb?*' is the reproof the poet seems to hear from his 'rigorous teachers' as he contemplates 'these anchorites', not 'as their friend, or child' but in 'pity and mournful awe' for a lost world.[29]

Spiridion (the name is taken from a Greek saint of the fourth century) is born Samuel Hebronius, a Jew, in the seventeenth century. He embraces Luther's Protestantism, and then through the study of Bossuet converts to Roman Catholicism, changes his name to Spiridion to mark having been illuminated by the Spirit, and founds in Italy an abbey of which he is prior until his death. His spirit still haunts it. Buried with him is a secret manuscript of inestimable worth that he has left to his disciple, Fulgence. Fulgence, dying in his turn, leaves the manuscript to Alexis, who in the course of the novel is transmitting its message, along with large slices of autobiography, to the novice, Angel. The novel no doubt embodies memories of convent life, as Pommier says, along with elements of Radcliffean gothic. The excitement of all this might seem to be minimal, but Sand manages to keep up considerable suspense, as we wonder what on earth the manuscript will turn out to be. Father Alexis' story is one of disgust with the venality of his fellow monks, disillusionment with Roman Catholicism, and recourse to scientific research as the way to ultimate truth. But science gives him a kind of burnout of the heart, a spiritual dryness. He is occasionally blessed by visitations from the sanctified presence of Spiridion, and alternately desolated by his absence. When the novice Angel receives visitations from Spiridion, Alexis realizes that Angel is the next elect, to whom the secret must be passed. We discover that the holy Spiridion was in fact given to heresies—Spinozism, pantheism, perhaps atheism. He nevertheless carried on outward observance in the abbey, and arrived at a positive faith in progressive evolution. (The life of Spiridion is in fact a little allegory of the history of religion, ending in nineteenth-century doubt and resolution.) Reason and science, Spiridion discovers, are only *provisional*, and open to all humankind: we are *all* prophets, all in search of the 'word of life and the spirit of truth.' Alexis himself, in studying the spirit, abjures his Roman Catholic faith, and then in the next phase finds he is no longer Christian. And yet he has a religion: 'a belief full of desire and hope in the Divinity, an ineradicable sentiment of the just and unjust, a great respect for all religions and all philosophies, the love of the good, and the need for the true.'[30]

There is in the book a recurrent castigation of 'ignorance and imposture,' and a sanctification of 'l'esprit d'examen et de révolte'— freedom of thought and action. The revered names which appear from time to time throughout are Socrates, Epictetus, Plato, Jesus, Abélard, Thomas à Kempis, Luther. The Christian religion, it is said, was irreproachable at first, but now, institutionalized, is part of the establishment force of aristocratic power and represssion. Philosophy and science have invalidated it, and we await a new temple and a new gospel.

The novel bears a remarkable resemblance to Carlyle's *Sartor Resartus*, although it is very different in kind. Like *Sartor* it is a story of spiritual crisis, recovery, and anticipation of a new gospel. It is full of the Germanic ideas that Carlyle also borrowed, of myths as essential religious poetry and the religious value of symbols and metaphors. While it is a farrago of post-Comtean, post-Herderian religious thought and gothic nightmares and fainting spells, it abounds also in Sand's characteristic luminous eloquence: 'Je me demandais ce que je ferais de mon coeur. . . . on a des immenses désirs . . . immenses besoins.'[31]

Alexis's scientific endeavors have left him spiritually incapacitated, and he is impeded in his efforts to retrieve from Spiridion's tomb, under the stone marked HIC EST VERITAS, the document that will pass on the secret of unspeakable value for the future. During a time of plague he goes through a crisis and is expelled from the abbey. He joins a hermit devoted to the care of plague victims. (This turn of events conveniently gets him out-of-doors so that he can benefit from ecstatic communion with the Nature that George Sand herself was communing with on her journey to Majorca with Chopin.) Nature and concern for his fellow man melt Alexis' science-frozen heart, and he returns to the abbey and prepares to die. Young Angel succeeds in retrieving from the tomb the treasure of Spiridion, *one* manuscript in the first edition of 1839, *three* manuscripts in the version that Arnold and Renan read. Angel and the aged Alexis peruse them, passing them on, in turn, to us.

The first manuscript turns out to be the Gospel of John in the hand of the great Joachim of Flora, with parts of it highlighted in coloured inks:

> In the beginning was the Word, and the Word was with God, and the Word was God. . . . The hour cometh, when ye shall neither in this mountain, nor yet at Jerusalem, worship the Father. . . . But the hour cometh, and now is, when the true worshippers shall worship the Father in spirit and in truth. . . . Is it not written in your law: I said ye are all gods?[32]

It will be noted that these texts suggest, first, the original mystic vision of John; second, an idea of religion developing to something more spiritual; and third, a text that might be taken as anti-supernaturalist, or humanist-democratic: all people are as gods.

The second document turns out to be a copy of the heretical *Introduction to the Eternal Gospel* of 1260 written by the hand of the celebrated John of Parma, disciple of Joachim of Flora. 'Religion has three epochs . . . the reign of the Father—the Mosaic, the reign of the Son—the Christian . . . the reign of the Holy Spirit, in which men will have no need of sacraments and will render to the Supreme Being a purely spiritual worship.'[33] Alexis notes that this seems to be as the Gospel of John predicted.

The third document is the work of Spiridion himself, and tells of his visions of Jesus. Jesus told him to discard the first three gospels, which were for their time only, and keep only John, the fourth. Jesus also revealed to him the writing of Joachim of Flora:

> Christianity must have three epochs, and the three epochs are accomplished. . ., the first from the origin and growth of the Church to Hildebrand in the eleventh century. . ., the second from Abélard to Luther and Bossuet—the reign of freedom of inquiry. It finishes Christianity, and then commences the era of a new religion. Let us not look for absolute truth in the literal application of the Gospels, but the revelations of all humanity that has gone before us. The three principles of human existence are *activity*, *love*, and *science*; each one who comes into the world receives all three as a child of God. The more we manifest ourselves in all three simultaneously, the more we approach divine perfection. Men of the future, to you it is reserved to realize this prophecy, if God is in you. It will be the work of a new revelation, a new religion, a new society, a new humanity. This religion will not abjure the spirit of Christianity but will do away with the forms. . . . It will continue the work of Christianity; that which Christianity has not understood, it will explain; that which Christianity has not dared, it will dare; that which Christianity has only undertaken, it will achieve.[34]

So ends Spiridion. The novel itself ends in a cataclysm of revolution, where the mob breaks into the abbey, and, as the insensate and ignorant agent of inexorable history, destroys the church and Alexis with it. So must the old pass, but the eternal gospel will be fulfilled.

Amongst all the impossible and often confused events and visions, there still shines forth that beautiful clarity of insight and expression that characterizes George Sand. Renan loved the book; Jean Pommier loves it. Renan said that George Sand was an 'Aeolian Harp of her century, vibrating to all the winds of the spirit'.[35] The image is charming even if it makes her out to be somewhat passive. What is astounding is the vigorous, active, broad reach of her intellect. *Spiridion* is a compendium of the free religious thought of the time. Pommier argues persuasively, moreover, that all the decisive elements of Renan's *Vie de Jésus* (1863) are here in Sand's book: the human Christ, the evolution of the human mind as the key to understanding the universe, the progressive realization of God on earth, and life after death or 'resurrection' as a mental process by which Socrates and Jesus are still 'alive' now in our lives—insofar as we know them still.

It will perhaps not seem surprising, when one remembers Arnold's religious concerns, that he reread *Spiridion* in 1882 with such engagement. The story-line may be a little troubled, but it provides a forum for quantities of pithy *logia*. He generally found her pithy: there are extracts from her *La Daniella* in the earliest extant *Note-Books*, of 1859, and sporadically thereafter, from a wide range of her works.

One of the things Renan loved in *Spiridion* was the re-creation of Joachim of Flora. Matthew Arnold was also, I think, very impressed. For in the so-called 'General Note-Books' of uncertain date, immediately following an extract from George Sand, he makes various transcriptions concerning Joachim.[36]

The Sand passage is from *L'Homme de neige* in French. I translate:

Do not be anxious or discouraged about your future. It will be fine if it is useful; for, look, I am going to give you advice quite opposed to that of the world. Others will say to you: Sacrifice everything to ambition. I say to you: Sacrifice, first of all, ambition, as the world understands it; that is, do not think of future or renown; go straight towards a single end, that of the enlightenment of your generation, no matter the condition or the means. . . .

As for the lost time that you regret, you are young enough to regain it amply. I also have been somewhat frivolous: and then after having spent my youth rather madly, I recovered myself, and I go ahead. I have a strong constitution, and so have you. I work twelve hours a day, and that is possible for anyone who is not frail or ill. Throw yourself into study, and let the incapable search for pleasure. They will not find it where they think, and you will find it where it is—that is, in peace of conscience and the exercise of noble faculties.

There follows a passage from Sainte-Beuve on Bonstetten:

Continual education, acquisition and renewal possible right up to the end of life!

These transcriptions in all likelihood are from 1882, and it is touching to see Arnold, at sixty, steadfast in his vocation. Next come a few lines from Bernouf's translation into French from Sanskrit, exhorting to *courage* and to *energy*, which will cultivate in one—Arnold underlines the French—'the fecund germs which the practice of duty will always leave in the heart of a being endowed with morality'. Then comes an unidentified French passage that he had previously written down in a Note-Book of 1860, and now recopies:

> There exists outside of the Church a certain number of souls who have conserved a very lively sense of the moral impoverishment of our time, and have kept the desire to remedy it. Where the School of the *Encyclopédie* saw nothing but an incoherent mass of barbarous superstitions, these have recognized the greatest religion which has ever aspired to make the happiness of the world.

Quite likely this is George Sand, but has not been identified. Then comes a paragraph from Rousseau asserting a need not only for virtue but also for a certain principle on which to base it. And then, again George Sand, this time identified as coming from her *Histoire de ma vie*:

> When you annihilate in yourself the personality that aspires to terrestrial joys, a celestial joy penetrates you, and absolute and delicious confidence inundates your heart with a well-being impossible to describe.

It is at this point that Arnold transcribes the long Latin passage labelled 'Joachim of Flore (died 1207)', from the *Acta Sanctorum*. It gives the doctrine of the Joachimite three stages. The next extracts reflect, as it were, some research on the matter: a Latin passage from the Proceedings of the Council of Arles of 1260 which condemned the Joachimite doctrine, then the passage from the Vulgate Revelation from which John of Parma developed his idea of *Evangelium Aeternum*, or 'Eternal Gospel' (in the King James Version):

> And I saw another angel fly in the midst of heaven, having the everlasting gospel to preach unto them that dwell on the earth, and to every nation, and kindred, and tongue, and people.
>
> (Revelation 14, 6)

There is yet another Latin transcription from the *Directorium Inquisitorum* of 1585 which describes and rejects the heresy.

These transcriptions in Arnold's notebooks imply a keen interest in and extensive meditation on the Joachimite historicism apparently introduced to him by Sand's *Spiridion*. They appear to be linked to her religious sense of dedication to a new era of equality; they would also connect with Arnold's own dedication—cooler, wittier, more urbane on the surface than George Sand's, but equally earnest in fact. Overall, the investigation of the Sand-Arnold connection reveals much about them both. Through his devotion to her, we must newly appreciate her humane breadth of interests and her heretofore neglected spirituality, and recognize in him a generous and enduring appreciation of her, untainted by any shadow of male condescension. A hundred years later, I think it can safely be said that her reputation is indeed growing, and Arnold's great regard for her challenges criticism.

Notes

[1] 'Count Leo Tolstoi' (1887) (*CPW* xi 282).

[2] 'George Sand' (1884) (*CPW* x 189).

[3] Patricia Thomson brings these together in *George Sand and the Victorians: Her Influence and Reputation in Nineteenth-Century England* (New York: Columbia University Press, 1977), 96. This is an excellent book, learned, readable, and full of insights. The chapter on Arnold, 'Arnold's "Days of Lélia" ' (90–120), is invaluable, and I have made use of it in this essay. Paul Blount's *George Sand and the Victorian World* (Athens: University of Georgia Press, 1970) is also useful, but not so extensive.

[4] 'K' was the family nickname for Arnold's much-loved older sister Jane Martha (b. 1 Aug. 1821).

[5] Quoted Thomson, 118. For the rest of the quotation see *Trilling* 381 and Introduction (p. 7).

[6] 'George Sand' (1877) (*CPW* viii 218).

[7] Thomson, 8.

[8] 'George Sand' (1877), loc. cit. 220.

[9] Thomson, 99.

[10] Iris Sells, *Matthew Arnold and France* (Cambridge, 1935; reprinted 1970), 36.

[11] 'Maurice de Guérin' (1863) (*CPW* iii 12–39).

[12] Francis Espinasse, *Literary Recollections* (London, 1893), 277; cited Thomson, 30.

[13] *Ward*, 12, quoted Thomson, 94.

14 'George Sand' (1877), loc. cit. 220.

15 Ibid., 219.

16 Letter of 24 February 1888 to Mrs. Coates (*Letters* ii 376).

17 'George Sand' (1877), loc. cit. 228.

18 Ibid., 220.

19 See Oscar Wilde, 'George Sand', *The Artist as Critic, Critical Writings of Oscar Wilde*, ed. Richard Ellmann (London, 1870), quoted Thomson, 207.

20 'Obermann Once More', ll. 323–4 (*Poems* 576).

21 Henri Bourdet-Guillerault, *George Sand: Ce qu'elle croyait* (Marseille: Editions Rijois, 1979).

22 Loc. cit. 9 (my translation, as throughout).

23 Ibid., 25.

24 'George Sand' (1877), loc. cit. 219. Arnold is quoting from *Journal d'un Voyageur pendant la guerre* (Paris, 1811), 119. See also *Note-books*, 277.

25 'Equality' (1878) (*CPW* viii 279).

26 *Spiridion*, Presentation de Georges Lubin (Var: Editions d'aujourd'hui, 1976).

27 *Note-books*, 366–86.

28 Jean Pommier, *George Sand et la rêve Monastique: Spiridion* (Paris: Librairie A. G. Nizet, 1966). Bourdet-Guillerault, in his study of Sand's beliefs, draws on Pommier.

29 'Stanzas from the Grande Chartreuse', ll. 67–84 (*Poems* 304–5).

30 *Spiridion*, ed. cit. 120.

31 Ibid., 175–6.

32 Ibid. 252–3. *John* i 1, iv 22–3, x 35; *Psalms* 82, 6. Authorized version, but I have added *all* to the last sentence: George Sand has, 'Vous êtes tous des dieux'.

33 *Spiridion*, ed. cit. 254–5.

34 Ibid., 256–9.

35 Quoted Pommier, i.

36 The passages that follow are all from *Note-books*, 485–9. I discovered, too late for this essay, a very learned and delightful book: *Joachim of Fiore and the birth of the Eternal Evangel in the Nineteenth Century* (Oxford: Clarendon Press, 1987), by Marjorie Reeves and Warwick Gould, reviewed by Frank Kermode (*TLS*, 25 September–1 October 1987; 1054–5).

A Working Isaiah: Arnold in the Council Office

VINCENT L. TOLLERS

What did Matthew Arnold do for thirty-five years in that grinding job as an Her Majesty's Inspector?[1] We have some help with the answer from as early as 1898, when Joshua Fitch wrote on the educational influences of both Thomas and Matthew Arnold, and we have had of course the recent work of David Hopkinson and Park Honan.[2] Little needs to be added to studies by R. H. Super and others about Arnold's foreign travel and his publications related to British education. Three times he travelled to central and southern Europe to study their primary and secondary educational systems: in 1859, on the Newcastle Commission; in 1865–66, on the Taunton Commission; and, in 1885–86, on the Cross Commission. These trips led to his educational publications including *The Popular Education of France*, *A French Eton*, 'The Twice-Revised Code', and *Schools and Universities on the Continent*— and a host of shorter works.

But a good deal of not so widely known additional information from the Public Record Office (PRO) helps to place in perspective the view held in some quarters that Arnold was invariably indifferent or hostile about his everyday work. If his work patterns are to be understood, Arnold must be seen in the context of the shifting educational policies that largely determined his daily routine. In an attempt to assemble some of the facts and statistics which affected his work in the inspectorate, it seems well to look at the general state of education, first from 1833 to 1862, then from 1862 to 1870, and finally, from 1870 to his retirement in 1886.

In the first of these periods, then, one can start by pointing out that state-supported education began on August 17, 1833, when the government allocated £30,000 to build schools in England, Scotland, and Wales to support religious groups that educated poor elementary pupils. After 1839, the grant was conditional on the approval of Her Majesty's Inspectors (HMIs), who had the power to deny grants. To aid schoolmasters as well as to insure a new generation of teachers, an 1846 Minute of the Committee on Council for Education started a work-study pupil-teacher system in which schoolmasters trained thirteen to eighteen year-old indentured males and females. (Educational policy was legislated in the Minutes of this Committee of the Privy Council until the government formed the Education Department in 1856.) The 1846 Minute shifted the primary workload of the HMI from inspecting sites to examining staff and pupils.

Once the inspector certified the schoolmasters and examined the school log book, he began oral and written examinations of the younger pupils, class by class, and pupil-teachers, individually. The girls had to prove their practical needlework skills to a qualified seamstress whose opinion Arnold always accepted; religious examination was deferred to a dissenting clergyman designated by the managers. Over their five years of indenture, pupil-teachers took a series of examinations. For example, inspectors had to examine fifth-year pupil-teachers in 'the composition of an essay on some subject connected with the art of teaching; the rudiments of algebra; syntax, etymology, and prosody; the use of globes or in the geography of the British Empire and Europe; Holy Scriptures, liturgy, and catechism; and the ability to give a gallery lesson and to conduct the instruction of the first class in any subject selected by the inspector.'[3] Upon passing this test, pupil-teachers could move to the next level by passing either the examination to be a certified assistant teacher or for the exhibition (Queen's scholarship) leading to a student grant in one- or two-year programs in one of the thirteen Training Colleges. Arnold generally spent over a week every December administering these examinations in four of the colleges.[4]

The largest elementary schools could enroll up to 600 boys and 600 girls, taught by a schoolmaster or schoolmistress supported by a maximum of thirty pupil-teachers and some certified assistant teachers.[5] However, during Arnold's early inspecting years, most schools were not this large. A Minute of May 4, 1859 set the maximum of pupil-teachers in an institution: forty students for each pupil-teacher and no more than four of them for each master or mistress.[6] Rural schools having fewer than ninety scholars were not required to have pupil-teachers.[7]

In early 1851, Arnold was at a crossroads. For four years, he had spent most of his work day reading, for as the private secretary to Lord Lansdowne, the President of the Privy Council, he had had few duties. Later, Arnold said that these were among his most intellectually productive years. Still, twenty-eight and single, he was not getting on. Both his mother and Ralph W. W. Lingen, his Balliol friend and the Secretary of Education, prodded him to be an inspector. Perhaps even more compelling was Arnold's need to earn more money, for Frances Lucy (Flu) Wightman would not marry him until he had a decent income.[8]

So he stepped forward to be an HMI—a decision that shaped his future. In 1851, this imaginary job description would have fitted Arnold:

> *Position Available*: A university-educated man required to work as 1 of 20 of Her Majesty's Inspectors for the Council on Committee of Education. Annual duties: as 1 of 3 HMIs of dissenting (often poor) schools in the midland counties of England and Wales, to inspect sites for building or improving elementary schools and to examine schoolmasters and schoolmistresses, pupil-teachers, and pupils; to examine applicants for exhibitions (Queen's scholarships), certified assistant teachers, and lecturers in 4 Training Colleges; to write a General Report during 2 weeks of relief from inspecting. Considerable travel necessary. Salary: £200 per annum plus per diem.

On April 14, 1851, Arnold was appointed, and on June 10, he and Flu married. Four months later, on October 15, 1851, Arnold wrote to her from Manchester in a mood of determined optimism about his goals:

> I think I shall get interested in the schools after a little time; their effects on the children are so immense, and their future effects on civilising the next generation of the lower classes, who, as things are going, will have most of the political power of the country in their hands, may be so important. It is really a fine sight in Manchester to see the anxiety felt about them, and the time and money the heads of their cotton-manufacturing population are willing to give them. In arithmetic, geography, and history the excellence of the schools I have seen is quite wonderful, and almost all the children have an equal amount of information; it is not confined, as in schools of the richer classes, to the one or two cleverest boys. We shall certainly have a good deal of moving about; but we both like that well enough, and we can always look forward to retiring to Italy on £200 a year. I intend seriously to see what I can do in such a case in the literary way that might increase our income. But for the next three or four years I think we shall both like it well enough.[9]

Park Honan dismisses Arnold's early inspectorate colleagues as dilettantes: 'In England the state merely allocated a small sum of money each year to schools run by churches and charities—and employed a few clergymen, dons, and philosophers to see how it was spent. These were the HMIs.'[10] However, as schools and pupils mushroomed, the 'clergymen, dons, and philosophers' were eased aside by hard-working, dedicated professionals, many of whom would rise to prominence. For instance, in 1877 Arnold himself recruited Joshua G. Fitch, the Principal of the Borough Road Training School who finished his career as Chief Inspector of Training Colleges. Similarly, W. B. Hodgson, Arnold's immediate superior, moved to the Chair of Economic Science at the University of Edinburgh in 1871.

While Arnold often wrote about his long, hard days as an inspector and, starting with his middle years, pressing financial need, he seldom looked for another position. He appears to have seriously tried three times: in 1856, he sought, then declined, a school inspectorship on the island of Mauritius; in 1866, he lost to another applicant as a charity commissioner; and in 1867, he lost to an inside candidate for the Librarianship of the House of Commons.[11] Though many of the poems he wrote in the early 60s suggest how constricting he found the life and at how hard a price his serenity was won, by forty-five, Arnold seemed content to stay in a career he was to pursue for a total of thirty-five years.[12]

Almost immediately after he was appointed an inspector, his assigned region began to shrink and his case load increase. In 1851, Arnold inspected 104 dissenting schools; in 1854, he visited about the same number, but his district was reduced in size when a fourth HMI was appointed for nonconformist schools.[13] Honan notes that the next year, in 1855, Arnold examined a whopping '173 "elementary schools" and 117 "institutions", 368 pupil-teachers and 97 certified teachers, as well as 20,000 pupils'.[14] Because the few dissenting schools were so scattered in the early 1850s, Arnold found it convenient to rent quarters when he travelled extensively—sometimes taking Flu with him and other times leaving her in rented lodging or in London with her parents. The 1854 case-load shift was the first of almost yearly reductions of Arnold's district. As early as 1856, Greater London became the centre of his inspecting.

Then in 1858, the Arnolds moved to their first permanent home, 2 Chester Square, near Flu's parents in fashionable Belgravia in London's West End. After ten years there, in 1868, they moved with their five children and menagerie of pets to Byron House, Harrow. From Arnold's July 29, 1868 reply to Charles Eliot Norton, who wanted to rent Byron House when the Arnolds were on holiday, we can only be amazed at the number of servants Arnold left behind: a gardener, a man-servant, a cook, and two housemaids. At his next home, he would cut back on a lavish lifestyle which was clearly beyond his means.

Early in 1871, Arnold wrote to his mother: 'They are proposing for me a *perfect* district; *Westminster*, and a small rural district round Harrow. And I have made no application, said not a single word!'[15] We can only speculate that this move was linked to the Department's plan for him: on April 1, he was appointed Senior Inspector. Although his personal inspecting territory would shrink yet a little more in the 1880s, for the remaining fifteen years of his career it was confined to Metropolitan London and a small part of Middlesex.

In 1873, the Arnolds made their final move—to Pains Hill Cottage, Cobham, Surrey, on the western outskirts of London. Ten years after Arnold became an HMI, notes Richard D. Altick, England had 6,600 miles of railroads, and would add another 15,000 miles by the time of his death. De Quincey, writing when Arnold was a young man, timed the London-Glasgow mail coach at twelve miles per hour; this 'gave way by mid-century to the express train's forty or fifty.'[16] From Chester Square, Harrow, or Cobham, Arnold could reach the Council Office and most of his schools in an hour or so on the train, now swift and convenient transportation.

By 1862, the beginning of the second major administrative change in the Education Department, Arnold's letters show that he saw himself as far more than an obscure HMI buried in the administrative bowels of Whitehall—that he was well placed to achieve his goals. That year, Robert Lowe, the Vice-President of the Education Department (1859–64), successfully championed the much-hated 'payment by results' legislation in the House of Commons: for the next quarter century, Arnold had to attest that pupils and pupil-teachers met minimum attendance requirements and satisfactorily passed reading, writing, and arithmetic examinations before their schools earned annual grants.

While the public may have seen him as 'an aloof poet and obscure school inspector' who only with the publication of *Culture and Anarchy* (1869) would become 'the prophet of sweetness and light,'[17] Arnold seemed unconcerned—perhaps because those who counted knew better. This position is clear in a letter he wrote to Miss Davies, the Girton College educator, explaining why he should not be on the Taunton or Schools Inquiry Commission (1865): 'I myself have always held but one language—that, from the unpopularity of my notions real or supposed, I should compromise the Commission somewhat with the public, and had better not be on it. . . . I turn more and more towards indirect and gradual modes of action—such as literature.'[18]

Writing anonymously or pseudonymously (as 'A Lover of Light', etc.)[19] and refusing to speak publicly, Arnold instead exerted his influence through his easy, frequent access to a host of key political supporters of education such as James Kay-Shuttleworth (who functioned as Secretary of Education in the Privy Council, 1839–49), W. E. Forster (Vice-President of the Education Department, 1868–70, and Arnold's closest brother-in-law), and A. J. Mundella (Vice-President of the Education Department, 1880–5). Furthermore, Arnold regularly met and most likely conferred about important educational matters with his old Rugby and Oxford friends at the Atheneum Club or over dinner. This is clear from even the most cursory reading of his letters, Guthrie's dissertation, and the PRO documents. The club, close to the Council Office, was Arnold's frequent late afternoon haunt after he was elected to it in February, 1856, by Forster's nomination. To complete *A French Eton*, a manuscript which gave him considerable difficulty, for instance, he was there from eleven o'clock to three o'clock daily in mid-January, 1864.[20] Eleven o'clock was unusually early for Arnold, especially after he moved to Pains Hill Cottage.

Arnold's late afternoon routine after 1878, as evident from his correspondence, was to wait at the Atheneum for his train home. At the club, he talked with the top leaders of the nation, wrote, and read. Undoubtedly, old-boyism prevailed there between Arnold and his Balliol College friends who became Secretaries of Education: Lingen (Secretary from 1849 to 69) was Arnold's tutor; Sir Francis Sandford (1870–84) was two years his junior; and Patrick Cumin (1884–90) was a fellow Newcastle Assistant Commissioner and from 1868 to 1870, Forster's private secretary. Cumin most certainly did not treat his relationship with Arnold lightly. He wrote in his memoirs that Arnold was one of his two closest Oxford friends.[21] Arnold, therefore, had little need to directly appeal to the public; he had the decision-makers' ears. For instance, Kay-Shuttleworth received his permission to privately print and distribute to every MP a copy of 'The Twice-Revised Code', the attack on Lowe's Revised Code that Arnold anonymously published in *Fraser's* on March 5, 1862.

Arnold also had personal access to powerful men in education through his commercial and official departmental publications. For instance, he sent Gladstone a personal letter along with *A French Eton* and also instructed Macmillan to send copies of it to many influential people including H. A. Bruce, soon to succeed Lowe.[22] Another indication of his closeness to key individuals is found in his letter to his mother about meeting Bruce at the Atheneum. He wrote that Bruce told him not to be concerned about losing his job because of his damaging testimony when Lowe's doctoring of inspectors' reports led to a parliamentary hearing and his forced resignation; after all, Bruce reminded Arnold, Lingen was his friend.[23]

Under Queen Victoria, then, education became one of England's primary enterprises, and Arnold was at its geographical and political centre. These years of explosive changes are reflected in the rapidly increasing number of Education Department bureaucrats. Hundreds of inspectors were hired to examine thousands of new schools built for millions of new pupils.

Tables rarely make interesting reading, but the one which appears below, compiled from intermittent, yet, detailed correspondence between various Secretaries of Education and Treasury, is worth printing because it does show the acute staffing pressures Education faced to fund worthy schools. Between 1848 and 1864, for instance, the number of inspectors increased five-fold—and that number was small compared with later years. By 1868, the combined number of HMIs and assistant HMIs in the country was 96; and by 1880, approximately 241. Expectedly, the number of clerks also skyrocketed. In 1857, there were 37; on July 6, 1876, the total was 60 clerks plus 100 to 120 man writers and 20 to 30 boy writers. By 1879, there were 253 clerks and men and boy writers.[24] It should be clear from the table that during Arnold's years as an HMI, the Education Department grew from a handful of amateurs to a small army of bureaucrats.

Department of Education Staffing: 1848–1880

	Clerks	Men-boy Writers	HMIs	Asst. HMIs	Temp. HMIs
1848			12		
1851			20		
1857	37				
1863			60		
1864	54				
1868			75	21	
1871			76	26	63

	Clerks	Men-boy Writers	HMIs	Asst. HMIs	Temp. HMIs
1873			79	28	
1875			99	42	
1876	60	135†	116	62	
1877			123	74	
1878			125	84*	
1879	83	170	131	94	
1880			137	104	

† Average
* Estimated increase of ten Assistant HMIs based on surrounding data.

The Revised Code of 1862 profoundly changed Arnold's job. He, along with other inspectors and educators, hated the new law because it stipulated that grants be 'payments by results', based on detailed reports: only schools which passed all tests (attendance quotas, building inspection, and minimum competency levels) received lump-sum annual maintenance grants. And many didn't. In 1871, Arnold approved 31 of 60 new applications in three Westminster districts: St. Anne, Soho (4 of 20 passed), St. Clement Danes (4 of 8 passed), and St. George, Hanover Square (23 of 32 passed). As illustrated in the table, an increased bureaucracy was the high price the government paid for holding the purse and writing the law. Contrasting the former and current role of the inspector in his General Report of 1863, Arnold wrote:

> The whole school felt, under the old system, that the prime aim and object of the Inspector's visit was, after insuring the fulfillment of certain sanitary and disciplinary conditions, to test and quicken the intellectual life of the school. . . . The new examination . . . takes up much more time and it throws upon him a mass of minute detail, and severely tasks hand and eye to avoid mistakes.[25]

The examination burden was eased somewhat for Arnold by one and sometimes two assistant inspectors who were assigned to him after 1864: Thomas Healing (1864–82) and Charles Myhill (1882–6). Also, from 1870–71, John W. Judd served as Arnold's special assistant

HMI for inspecting buildings when so many new schools came into the system under the Forster Act. Arnold praised Healing from the time he began working under him, as we can see from his letter to his mother.[26] Their cordial relationship continued through the years when Healing became an HMI; later he was a key speaker at Arnold's retirement party. Both he and Myhill helped Arnold in several ways. They took over the paperwork of scheduling from 150 to 200 annual inspections and administering examinations, and orally examined about half of the pupils.[27]

Yet, Arnold always had the task of personally examining the elementary schoolmasters, schoolmistresses, and pupil-teachers in addition to the Training College scholarship and certified assistant-teacher candidates and lecturers. Under the Revised Code, the Council Office set and prepared the examinations; Arnold graded them, and the assistant took care of getting them from and returning them to the department.

The first step in the examination process began weeks in advance— setting the inspection date. The PRO files show that Arnold was constantly juggling schedules—primarily to accommodate the managers, to shift cases temporarily to other inspectors while he was on his trips abroad, or to transfer cases among the HMIs in realigned areas.[28] After 1862, Arnold or his assistant first had to inspect a newly-proposed site; then, Arnold had to recommend the number of seats and the grade levels for the school; and finally, he had to remain in touch with Council Office administrators responsible for site planning, cost and usage-level estimates, and specifications.[29]

But most of Arnold's work through the 60s consisted of personally inspecting existing schools. Each return visit began with an inspection of the premises to certify that the building was 'healthy, properly lighted, drained, and ventilated, supplied with offices, and containing in the principal schoolroom at least 80 cubical feet of internal space for each child in average attendance.'[30] Once the site met physical requirements, Arnold had to determine the average number of pupils regularly attending to ascertain if the school had a sufficient space allocation. In a letter to Lady de Rothschild on March 15, 1864, he mentions one roster problem he had:

> Instead of finding everything perfectly prepared for me, as it was in Bell Lane [the school she sponsored], I have to go through every schedule myself, correcting the errors and supplying the omissions of the managers and teachers. Imagine the pleasure of finding out

for oneself from each of 500 boys what his father is; and if, as generally happens, he is a tradesman, of finding out besides whether he is a small or great tradesman, and how many people he employs! Such is inspecting at present.[31]

Using a flood of new, detailed forms (Form X, the major one, was eight pages long), Arnold had to inspect even more carefully each person in every specified category. Schoolmasters and school-mistresses were tested for their competency in basic English history, basic British geography, arithmetic (neatly written and accurate), English composition, grammar, spelling, and school management.[32] The schoolmaster was required to report on the teachers' 'character, conduct, and attention to duty'; the inspector, to report on the efficiency of the school's 'organization, discipline, and instruction', the pupil-teachers' 'conditions of indenture', and 'types and adequacy of supervision'.[33]

After each visit, Arnold would take away the written examinations. Following the Revised Code procedure, he would read them and 'write only P (pass) on writing and arithmetic papers', and then forward the papers to the Council Office. While he observed during the Lowe hearings that the Council Office had tampered with the findings of other inspectors, only once did anybody try to change his. Three years before Arnold retired, Sandford asked him to revise his recommendations on two schools he inspected, citing new grant administration policy. Arnold replied: 'No change to make. Surely the line indicated in the Circulars is the line which any prudent inspector would naturally have followed in general. But it is impossible to give *good* for class-subjects as a matter of course. It would be better that the Department should allow the full grant as a matter of grace than that the inspector should describe as *good* what is certainly not more than *fair* at the very utmost.'[34]

The final major legislative change that affected Arnold's activities was the Education (or Forster) Act of 1870. For nineteen years, he had inspected only the dissenters' schools; now he was responsible for all schools in the jurisdiction of the London School Board—dissenters, Church of England, Roman Catholic, and non-sectarian. Fitch wrote that Arnold's territory 'was practically limited to one of the easiest divisions of the metropolis—the borough of Westminster—a district so well provided with voluntary denominational schools that for a long time there was in it only one school provided by the London School Board.'[35]

By 1871, this imaginary job description fitted Arnold:

Position Available: Senior Inspector in the Education Department. Administrative and inspecting duties under the Education Act of 1870: to supervise 8 HMIs and their assistant and temporary HMIs in Metropolitan District schools; to recommend new or improved building sites under the London School Board, especially for middle class pupils in local (non-sectarian) schools; annually, to examine school sites, schoolmasters and schoolmistresses, certified assistant teachers, pupil-teachers, and pupils in Westminster schools, and to write a General Report every second year; annually, to inspect sites and examine applicants for exhibitions (Queen's scholarships), certified assistant teachers, and lecturers in 4 Training Colleges; 2 assistants provided. Little travel outside of London required. Considerable paperwork necessary. £50 bonus for clearing cases by August 1.

After 1871, Arnold's workload seems to have increased—though its nature changed. Essentially, he traded the primary duties of personally inspecting schools for administrative work. Fitch, who joined him in 1877, notes that Arnold's strengths and weaknesses must have been severely tested:

The details of administration, the framing of syllabuses and schedules, and the laying down of the legal conditions under which the public grant should be assessed and distributed, were tasks not to his mind. But when questions of principle were involved, he was frequently consulted, and we who were his colleagues received from him at times very weighty and practical suggestions.[36]

Although Healing and Judd relieved him in the field, he had still, to supervise them. In 1871–72, they inspected 132 new schools: Arnold either passed or rejected applications based on their findings, only occasionally requiring them to come back with more information.[37] At times, Arnold needed to sort out their territorial limits. Once Judd noted for him on the report for the Westminster Regimental School, Wellington Barracks, Bird Cage Walk: 'A second school of some kind at the Wellington Barracks. No return. Both reported on by Inspectors from the War Office.' Arnold replied: 'See War Office Reports,' and later, 'I have sent in the Return for this Parish.'[38]

As the immediate supervisor of Healing and Judd, Arnold also dealt with their personal concerns. For instance, Sandford wrote Arnold on

July 18, 1882 to tell Healing that he had 36 working days for vacation and private business per year.[39] The even broader control of the Council Office over the private lives of the assistant inspectors was apparent when Charles Myhill wanted to move to a less expensive home in a suburb. Arnold wrote the Council Office: 'I suppose there is no objection to Mr. Myhill's proposed change of abode?' The next day 'P' denied the request: 'It cannot be accepted. It is too distant from his work, and would, also, be distinctly more expensive. If he wishes to move, it would seem that some places, e.g., about Clapham, Buxton, Dulwich, should be chosen.' Arnold tersely responded: 'Communicated to Mr. Myhill.' Not to be daunted, on October 9, Myhill explained to Arnold why he wanted to live in Wimbledon: it offered easy access to his assigned schools in the Vauxhall and Waterloo districts of Westminster, lower rent, and the same travel expenses. This time Arnold wrote directly to A. G. Sykes, the Assistant Secretary, indicating that he supported Myhill's application. When Sykes niggardly replied that 'My Lords will not object to Wimbledon,' Arnold replied: 'Communicated to Mr. Myhill who will return it to C.O.'[40]

After 1871, an extensive part of Arnold's job was to oversee assistants assigned to other inspectors; the Council Office required him to re-assign assistants when their HMI didn't need them.[41] After 1883, when he was Chief Inspector, he also supervised eleven Westminster District HMIs, and by extension, their assistants. Later, when these assistants wanted to change residences, Arnold decided if they could.[42]

Meanwhile, the number of his cases increased relentlessly. New tasks included finding classrooms for boys and girls not enrolled in parochial schools. Sandford wrote William Law, Secretary of the Treasury, that 'each inspector now [has] 200 departments to visit each year.'[43] Especially after the London School Board was created in 1870, Arnold spent many hours on school construction problems. For example, when the clerk, S. H. Croad, requested permission to move and enlarge the James Street Buckingham Gate School from 484 to 600 students, Arnold decisively recommended:

> The St. James School is an old established school, with a large connexion, and should be continued though it lose its present premises.
> I think the Board, when they build, may purposely build for 600. There is a considerable population around the old school, and the only other school quite near is a R. C. school, St. Edmund's.

Victoria Street is a channel which the children do not cross, and Pye Street, in [the] AE [district], will not do much to feed a school in AC. But there are abundant means in AE for meeting the requirement of Rye Street, when they arise. In replacing the St. James St. School, the Board must not travel far from where that school now stands.[44]

Based on Arnold's thinking, Hodgson wrote Sandford: 'On the strength of this report, wd approve this proposal to provide addl award for 116 ch[ildren].'[45] Then in July, when Croad requested permission to foreclose on thirteen cottages in Castle Lane, James Street, to build the school, Henry F. Pooley, in charge of building, asked Arnold: 'Do you approve this situation chosen?' And he simply replied: 'Yes.'[46]

Throughout his career, Arnold was obliged to deal with local politics in education, but the charged atmosphere of the School Board caused him great grief. In a letter to Hodgson, he shrewdly commented about the forces to consider in what was ultimately a fifteen-month hassle in 1881–82 surrounding the closing of the St. James Offeratory School and the expansion of the Pulteney Schools:

> I called the other day to speak to you about the proposed enlargement of the Pulteney Schools. The Board of Works are at last about to proceed with their new street through Soho. The clergy allege that the demolitions will remove a large number of the working class. But at present the Board are bound by the stipulation that they shall re-house, in the locality, as many of the working class as they displace. They are trying, however, to get this stipulation removed. I don't think they will succeed; but if they do, the working class population will be reduced, I am told, by more than 6000. I think we may wait and see whether the Board succeed in getting rid of the re-housing proviso; if they do not, I think the enlargement of the Pulteney Schools should be allowed.[47]

Apparently new housing was found, because on June 24, 1882, Croad wrote that the School Board recommended enlarging the Pulteney School.[48] Almost immediately, Miss Simcox from the School Board complained to Mundella that the Bedfordbury School was a better site. So, again Hodgson asked Arnold for his opinion. He replied on July 1: 'I think you are right in supposing that [the Westminster] J [ward] is not likely to feed the Pulteney School much. I think we should wait and see whether the locality shows growth of school population. At present there are no needs which the actual schools cannot with a little management fairly meet.' Armed with this opinion, on August 11, Cumin drafted a letter to Miss Simcox for Mundella's approval.[49] He granted it, and the issue was closed.

On August 8, 1884, Arnold became Chief Inspector, one of ten in the country. While the title changed, his duties remained fundamentally the same. Nevertheless, even from this level he resisted administrative pressures, especially from people who seemed to duplicate memos with glee. The PRO files include numerous memos from Charles W. Merrifield, a nitpicking examiner, who all too quickly prodded Arnold and those he supervised to be more prompt about returning their cases. Yet, Arnold's replies seldom showed irritation. Typically, to Merrifield's 'You have only reported on one of your March schools as yet. Please see Circular (No. 15) of 18 January 1878,' Arnold replies, 'I have only four March schools inspected yet, of which the reports are not gone in (Enfield is sent today). My February cases extend into the middle of March.'[50]

However, Arnold was too often caught between the balky inspectors and hand-wringing examiners. For example, several times Merrifield faulted him for not submitting a cumulative report of the quarterly returns from the eight district inspectors and the senior inspectors posted in his division. Once, instead of responding to the examiner, Arnold hotly wrote to the secretary that as the inspectors were resisting, he couldn't complete his report until Cumin directed them to respond—and did no more. Two weeks later he still had not received the reports, but it is not clear what ever happened.[51] Nevertheless, Arnold could effectively play the middle man between the inspectors and the administration. When Mr. Helps, his Chelmsford HMI, wanted to print a thick geography examination, Arnold persuaded the hierarchy, after several exchanges, to give the answer he wanted to hear: no.[52]

During his final days as an inspector and the two years he lived after his retirement, Arnold continued to give his full measure to education. His third fact-finding visit to the Continent, only weeks before his retirement on April 30, 1886, was soon followed by a *Special Report*, and the only two lectures he gave in America were titled 'Some Aspects of Foreign Education.'[53] Despite his regular complaints about his grinding job as an HMI, Matthew Arnold devoted his life and writings to the pronouncement made six months after he first began as an inspector:

I think I shall get interested in the schools after a little time; their effects on the children are so immense, and their future effects on civilising the next generation of the lower classes, who, as things are going, will have most of the political power of the country in their hands, may be so important.

Notes

1 I must thank Mr. Arnold Whitridge, the Public Record Office, and Girton College, Cambridge, for permission to publish quoted correspondence. Thanks are also due to the National Endowment for the Humanities for a Travel to Collections grant, and SUNY College, Brockport, for a period of sabbatical leave during which I completed most of this research.

2 See Joshua Fitch, *Thomas and Matthew Arnold and Their Influence on English Education* (New York: Scribners, 1898: referred to below as Fitch); W. F. Connell, *The Educational Thought and Influence of Matthew Arnold* (London: Routledge, 1950); William Guthrie Bell, 'Matthew Arnold's Diaries, The Unpublished Items: A Transcription and Commentary,' (four volumes, unpublished dissertation, University of Virginia, 1957); Peter Smith and Geoffrey Summerfield, *Matthew Arnold and the Education of the New Order* (Cambridge: Cambridge University Press, 1969); David Hopkinson, 'Matthew Arnold's School Inspections', in *History Today* (29, 1979: referred to below as Hopkinson) 29–37, 98–105; R. H. Super, ed., *Democratic Education and Schools and Universities on the Continent* (*CPW* ii, iv); and Park Honan, *Matthew Arnold: A Life* (Cambridge: Harvard University Press, 1983).

3 *Reports on Elementary Schools, 1852–1882; by Matthew Arnold*, ed. Francis Sandford (London: Macmillan, 1889: referred to below as Sandford), 299.

4 Letter to George Smith, 15 December, 1869 (Copy at the University of Virginia).

5 According to the Minutes of December 10, 1851 and May 12, 1852, each one was equal to two pupil-teachers.

6 Sandford, 299.

7 *Reports on Elementary Education, 1852–1882; by Matthew Arnold*, ed. F. S. Marvin, new ed. (London: Eyre, 1910: referred to below as Marvin), 371.

8 *Manchester Guardian*, May 18, 1888; and Honan, 216–19.

9 *Letters* i 17.

10 Honan, 218.

11 For the first two positions, see Howard Bernard Leichman, 'Matthew Arnold's Correspondence: The American Visits, May 21, 1882 to September 19, 1886' (Unpublished dissertation, University of Washington, 1972: referred to below as Leichman), xix; for the last, see the ALS from Edmund Gosse to Arnold (British Library, f. 60488).

12 See, e.g., 'Worldly Place', *Poems* 528, and 3–7n 529.

13 Hopkinson, 33.

[14] Honan, 262.

[15] Letter to his mother, 31 January 1871 (*Letters* ii 48).

[16] Richard D. Altick, *Victorian People and Ideas* (New York: Norton, 1973), 78, 96.

[17] Hopkinson, 100.

[18] Letter to Miss Davies, 28 December 1864, Girton College, Cambridge.

[19] Often Arnold's comments on education appeared anonymously in periodicals; he used this pseudonym for several articles published in *The Pall Mall Gazette* and the *Daily News*.

[20] *CPW* ii 370.

[21] Leichman, 230.

[22] Copies of ALSs, June 10–18, 1864, at the University of Virginia.

[23] July 6, 1864, Balliol (Copy at the University of Virginia).

[24] Public Record Office, ED 23/71 and 72 (hereafter cited as PRO).

[25] Fitch, 182.

[26] April 13, 1864, Balliol (Copy at the University of Virginia).

[27] PRO ED 36/1.

[28] PRO ED 36/1.

[29] Marvin, 334, 369.

[30] Marvin, 341.

[31] *Letters* i 228.

[32] Marvin, 371.

[33] Marvin, 283–84.

[34] June 20, 1883, PRO ED 36/1.

[35] Fitch, 176–7.

[36] Fitch, 177.

[37] PRO ED 3/27 and 3/28.

[38] PRO ED 3/28 121a.

[39] PRO ED 36/1.

[40] August 19–October 12, 1883, PRO ED 36/1.

[41] PRO ED 36/1.

[42] January 16, 1885, PRO ED 36/1.

[43] June 1, 1883, PRO ED 23/71.

[44] PRO ED 14/16.

[45] March 24, 1880, PRO ED 14/16.

[46] July 13 and 17, 1880, PRO ED 21.

[47] August 5, 1881, PRO ED 14/16.

[48] PRO ED 14/16.

[49] PRO ED 14/16.

[50] March 27, 1878, PRO ED 36/1.

[51] Arnold ALSs to Cumin, October 13, 1883, and July 10, 1884, PRO ED 36/1.

[52] November 2–8, 1884, PRO ED 36/1.

[53] Leichman, xxii.

Appendix

In Utrumque Paratus (1849, 1877, 1881, 1885)

If, in the silent mind of One all-pure,
    At first imagined lay
The sacred world; and by procession sure
From those still deeps, in form and colour drest,
Seasons alternating, and night and day,   5
The long-mused thought to north, south, east, and west,
    Took then its all-seen way;

O waking on a world which thus-wise springs!
    Whether it needs thee count
Betwixt thy waking and the birth of things   10
Ages or hours—O waking on life's stream!
By lonely pureness to the all-pure fount
(Only by this thou canst) the colour'd dream
    Of life remount!

Thin, thin the pleasant human noises grow,   15
    And faint the city gleams;
Rare the lone pastoral huts—marvel not thou!
The solemn peaks but to the stars are known,
But to the stars, and the cold lunar beams;
Alone the sun arises, and alone   20
    Spring the great streams.

But, if the wild unfather'd mass no birth
    In divine seats hath known;
In the blank, echoing solitude if Earth,
Rocking her obscure body to and fro,   25
Ceases not from all time to heave and groan,
Unfruitful oft, and at her happiest throe
    Forms, what she forms, alone;

O seeming sole to awake, thy sun-bathed head
    Piercing the solemn cloud   30
Round thy still dreaming brother-world outspread!
O man, whom Earth, thy long-vext mother, bare
Not without joy—so radiant, so endow'd

(Such happy issue crown'd her painful care)—
    Be not too proud!   35

Oh when most self-exalted most alone,
    Chief dreamer, own thy dream!
Thy brother-world stirs at thy feet unknown,
Who hath a monarch's hath no brother's part;
Yet doth thine inmost soul with yearning teem.   40
—Oh, what a spasm shakes the dreamer's heart!
    'I, too, but seem.'

line 2 imagined) imagin'd *1849*

6 long-mused) long-mus'd *1849*

11 life's) Life's *1849*

12 fount) Fount *1849*

14 life) Life *1849*; remount!) ˜. *1849, 1877*

29 sun-bathed) sun-bath'd *1849*

33 joy-) ˜; *1849*; ˜, *1869*; endow'd) ˜—*1849*

39 part;) part- *1877, 1881*

41 —Oh,) O *1849*; ˜ *1877, 1881*; heart!) heart— —*1849*

42 *seem.'*) *seem!' 1849*

In Utrumque Paratus (1869)

If, in the silent mind of One all-pure
  At first imagined lay
The sacred world, and by procession sure
From those still deeps, in form and colour drest,
Seasons alternating and night and day,   5
The long-mused thought to north, south, east, and west,
  Took then its all-seen way;

O waking on a world which thus-wise springs!
  Whether it needs thee count
Betwixt thy waking and the birth of things   10
Ages or hours—O waking on life's stream!
By lonely pureness to the all-pure fount
(Only by this thou canst) the colour'd dream
  Of life remount!

Thin, thin the pleasant human noises grow,   15
  And faint the city gleams,
Rare the lone pastoral huts;—marvel not thou!
The solemn peaks but to the stars are known,
But to the stars, and the cold lunar beams;
Alone the sun arises, and alone   20
  Spring the great streams.

But if the wild unfather'd mass no birth
  In divine seats hath known;
In the blank, echoing solitude if Earth,
Rocking her obscure body to and fro,   25
Ceases not from all time to heave and groan,
Unfruitful oft, and, at her happiest throe,
  Forms, what she forms, alone;

O seeming sole to awake, thy sun-bathed head
  Piercing the solemn cloud   30
Round thy still dreaming brother-world outspread!
O man, whom Earth, thy long-vext mother, bare
Not without joy, so radiant, so endow'd
(Such happy issue crown'd her painful care)!
  Be not too proud!   35

Thy native world stirs at thy feet unknown,
  Yet there thy secret lies!

Out of this stuff, these forces, thou art grown,
And proud self-severance from them were disease.
O scan thy native world with pious eyes!   40
High as thy life be risen, 'tis from these;
  And these, too, rise.

Notes on editor and contributors

Miriam Allott is Emeritus Professor of English, London University, Honorary Fellow, Liverpool University. She edited *The Poems of John Keats* (1970) for Longman's Annotated Poets, and worked on the second edition (1979) of *The Poems of Matthew Arnold* (first edition by Kenneth Allott, 1965) in the same series. She has written articles on nineteenth-century and twentieth-century novelists and poets, and is currently working on a biography of Clough and preparing the *Faber Book of Poets on Poetry*. Her edition, in collaboration with Nicholas Shrimpton, of *Matthew Arnold: The Complete Poetical Works*, is shortly to appear from Oxford University Press.

Ruth apRoberts is Professor of English at the University of California at Riverside. She is the author of *Arnold and God* (University of California Press, 1984) and *The Ancient Dialect: Carlyle and Comparative Religion*, which is shortly to appear from the same press. Her shorter publications include essays on Jane Austen and on Biblical translation.

Bernard Beatty, Senior Lecturer in English at Liverpool University, is the author of *Byron's Don Juan* (Croom Helm, 1985) and editor of *Don Juan and Other Poems* (Penguin, 1987); he co-edited with R. T. Davies *Literature of the Romantic Period, 1780–1830* (1976) and is academic editor of the *Byron Journal*. His work in progress includes a study entitled *Split Religion*.

Philip Davis is a lecturer in English and Director of the M.A. course in Victorian Literature at Liverpool University. His first book was *Memory and Writing—from Wordsworth to Lawrence* (Liverpool University Press, 1983), and he has published a number of articles in *Stand Magazine* on the relation between writing and living. He has recently completed a book on Samuel Johnson.

John P. Farrell is Professor of English at the University of Texas. He is the author of *Revolution as Tragedy* (Cornell University Press, 1980). He has co-edited a special edition of *Victorian Poetry* for the Arnold Centenary.

Brian Nellist is Senior Lecturer in English at Liverpool University. He has edited *Milton's Poems 1645*, and has written articles on the romantic poets, including Shelley and Byron.

Nicholas Shrimpton teaches English at Lady Margaret Hall, Oxford. He has published articles on Shakespeare, Bunyan, Blake, Ruskin, and Dante.

Vincent L. Tollers is Professor of English at SUNY College at Brockport. His major publications include *A Bibliography of Matthew Arnold* (1974) and *The Bible in Its Literary Milieu* (1979). He was editor of *Literary Research* from 1976 to 1986, and is co-editing a special 'Religious Studies' issue of the *Bucknell Review* to appear in early 1989.